The ILLUSIONS of ANIMAL RIGHTS

by Russ Carman

Cover art by Lynn Larson

Edited by Gordy Krahn

Published by:

 **krause**
publications

700 East State St.   Iola, WI 54990
Telephone: (715) 445-2214

Library of Congress Catalog Number 90-62656
ISBN: 0-87341-159-5
Printed in the United States of America

***DEDICATED TO THE MEMORY OF FRANK CARMAN,
MY FATHER, MY TEACHER ... MY FRIEND.***

Special thanks to Janice Henke for her help in editing.
Without her help and encouragement this book would
have never been finished.
Thanks also to Steven and Kathy Greene for your faith
and encouragement.

About the Author

Russ Carman does not have the formal, advanced education of the schoolroom, but he has a Ph.D. in wildlife conservation experience, common sense and knowledge gleaned for astute observation and thoughtful perception. A lifelong outdoorsman and sportsman, he lives with his wife and two children in rural Pennsylvania, gaining his early knowledge of nature from being in the field with his father. Carman has been a trapper and hunter throughout his life.

In 1975, an assassination attempt was made on the life of then President Gerald E. Ford by one "Squeaky" Fromme. Upon a search of her apartment, a list of names was found that targeted various people for assissination. Russ Carman and his wife were on that list. The supposed "crime" warranting death was that he was a trapper.

The taking of animals for consumptive use has been recognized as a necessary wildlife management tool to control and maintain wilflife populations. Suddenly, however, Carman realized that this activity was deemed unacceptable by some and that he had been singled out for elimination for those practices. This event triggered an indepth study of the animal rights movement, its origins, directions and future in our society and its impact upon the hunter, trapper, farmer, biomedical community and other segments of our society.

The Illusions of Animals Rights is a product of Carman's attempt to understand a movement that professes a love of animals, but is transformed into a hate for humans. From the vantage point of one who has been a farmer, trapper, hunter and a businessman involved in wildlife matters, Carmam brings years of experience and observation to a thoughtful overview of the historical and current issues involved in the animal rights movement.

PREFACE

PREFACE

By all outward appearances I am a normal middle aged American male. I have a wife, two children and a pet dog named "Beau". I work hard, pay my taxes and help my boy with his school work. I lead a somewhat private, quiet and well-adjusted life in rural America.

But, in the eyes of some people, there lies beneath that normal exterior a dark and sinister personality, so horrible, so vile that they feel an obligation to banish me from this earth.

What is it about me that stirs the wrath of movie and T.V. stars, news reporters and little old ladies? Am I a wife beater or child abuser, a rapist, a murderer or even a pornographer? Is it possible that I'm an opponent of free speech or a free press?

No, I am proud to say, I am none of the above. But in the eyes of a growing number of Americans I have become the "big bad wolf" of modern fairy tales; a reckless destroyer of innocent creatures; a grim, blood soaked reminder of man's primal past; I am a hunter, trapper and one time livestock farmer.

As a young boy I trapped muskrats in a small swamp outside town, and from those meager beginnings has grown a love for trapping that remains with me until this very day.

Although the life of the trapper is fraught with hardship, fatigue, discouragement and even danger, I know of no other occupation that gives a man such a strong sense that he is a part of God's creation.

The trapper draws great satisfaction from being a part of nature, and to know and understand the workings of that force. He learns to predict the weather by observing the movement of animals. He learns to love the smells of nature that are offensive to modern men. The pungent "skunk-like" odor of fox, the sharp acrid odor of mink, the sweet musky odor of deer, are like fine perfume to the trapper, when carried by the pure air of the woods and fields.

Because of the hardships he must endure as a trapper, the hard work and long hours, through rain, snow and bone-chilling cold, he better understands the hardships animals must endure, and he stands in awe.

He appreciates the clean, fresh air, and the physical and mental strength that he draws from nature. He knows that to become a part of nature, his role therein must be a necessary one; that he cannot become a part of nature, unless he somehow benefits her.

Like the Indian before him, he understands the laws of nature, and through that understanding comes great respect, and yes . . . even love.

Being the only son of an avid hunter, I was exposed to the age-old tradition of hunting at a very early age. Like many boys and girls in rural America, I was just as excited about getting my first hunting license, as I was at receiving my driver's license.

Some of my fondest memories of my Dad are the shared experiences we had while hunting together. It was while we were hunting that he taught me how to recognize the flowering dogwood tree; how to tell the difference between the hard and soft maple; where to look for ginseng roots; and how to build a camp fire in the rain.

We stood together in silence as we viewed the beauty of nature; the flocks of geese flying south, the squirrels scurrying up and down the trees storing nuts for the winter, the curiosity of the chickadee as it watched us from a nearby tree.

He showed me also the ugly side of nature; the mangy scab-covered fox that had crawled under a stump to die, the raccoon that wandered around aimlessly, his eyes white in blindness, the countless rotted carcasses of deer that had split their pelvic bones on the ice after a winter ice storm and the grey fox staggering around in the madness of rabies.

When I was sixteen, my family moved to a dairy farm, and for seven years we lived the hard, but rewarding life of dairy farmers.

For the first thirty years of my life I remained a small speck of humanity in a huge world. Not especially moral, or immoral; not especially greedy, or charitable; not especially smart, or ignorant. I had a few friends, and no real enemies. I was viewed, by virtually all standards of society, as perfectly normal.

On Sept. 5, 1975, a young woman made an unsuccessful attempt to assassinate then President Ford. Officials searching her apartment, which she shared with another girl, found a list of the names of prominent business men, targeted for assassination . . . a death list. Although we were not business people at the time, both my name, and my wife's were on that list. Suddenly, I was no longer viewed, at least by a small number of radicals, as a normal American. It was my first hint of things to come.

Those two girls were Lynnette "Squeaky" Fromme, and Sandra Good, both members of the radical Charles Manson cult, which was responsible for the murder and mutilation of actress Sharen Tate and the Labiancas.

When I received a phone call from the F.B.I. and was informed of the possible danger I faced from this cult, the thought was so outlandish that I shrugged it off as some kind of clever, but vicious, practical joke. Unfortunately, a few days later I received a letter from these two girls that had been mailed before they were apprehended. The content was so bizarre and sadistic, that I knew it was the work of a seriously disturbed mind.

As an officer of the Pennsylvania Trappers Association, I was considered by this group to be a cruel exploiter of nature, a sadistic murderer of innocent animals. For my evil behavior against nature, they threatened to tie us up, cut off our ears and lips, stick forks in our bellies and watch them wave in the wind. I knew at that moment that I suddenly had enemies . . . very brutal enemies. I had no way of knowing at the time, that my list of enemies would continue to grow.

The F.B.I. warned me to keep this death threat quiet for fear that other radical groups would pick up the banner. Little did I know that the seeds of a world-wide move-

8

ment had already been sown, or that this radical idea of animal rights would soon become so pervasive in our society. How could I know that I would soon become the victim of vicious slander and harassment that could almost be compared to the harassment of the Jews in the early years prior to World War II?

To say that the animal rights movement has left hunters, trappers and livestock farmers in a state of bewilderment would be putting it mildly indeed. After thousands of years of plying our trades, as an accepted part of society, we have suddenly become the victims of harassment, terrorism, slander and hate.

This book has grown out of my personal attempts to understand this phenomenon. The first question I had to face, very unexpectedly I might add, was how some peoples' professed love and compassion for animals could so easily be transformed into a hatred for humans . . . any humans.

The next question I had to answer, was how an ideology, considered so radical just a few short years ago, could be embraced and accepted by such a rapidly growing number of people.

Last of all, I had to answer the question of how a very small group of animal rights leaders, the great majority of whom cannot boast of an educational background or experience in animal husbandry or wildlife management, could gain so much raw power at all levels of society. Politicians rush to legislate the new "morality," movie and television stars become almost hysterical in their devotion to so-called animal rights, valuable television time is devoted to the evils of hunting and trapping and the fur coat is claimed to be the symbol of everything that is sick and perverted in our society.

The American animal rights "movement" has become a growth industry with a donated tax-free income estimated by different sources to reach 100 million dollars a year.

It is a business which makes its money by attacking trappers who individually make less than a thousand dollars a year from their industry, hunters who make no money from their sport and farmers who are going bankrupt in record numbers.

It may be a reflection of our times that an industry which produces no material wealth grows rich and powerful, while the industries being attacked, which produce billions of dollars for the American economy, struggle to survive.

What kind of appeal does "animal rights" provide that it causes society to ignore biologists, doctors, scientists, wildlife experts and highly educated professionals in animal husbandry, in favor of the opinions of movie stars, television critics, ideologue and even rock stars? What kind of appeal could be so strong that it causes people to literally bite the hands that feed them, and reject the wealth of our nation?

In the following pages I have made a careful and informed evaluation of the animal rights movement, the development of its ideology, how it is affecting the lives of humans all over the world and what it promises for the future.

This is a book written in two parts, about two different groups of people holding totally opposite moral and ethical views concerning animals. It is about the struggle between these two groups which will ultimately decide who will control the future of our animals. Should they be utilized as a source of our national riches, or should they be set free? Is it possible to return them to a nature that has become so dominated and altered by man, or should we continue to manage and control them? These are the questions Americans are being asked to decide.

In the following pages I have addressed these questions by examining the roots of the animal rights movement, as well as the basic foundations on which our present animal-use systems have been built.

Although very few people in the United States fully understand the total concept of the animal rights ideology, it is an idea that has the power to eventually affect every American. Because of our powerful and influential international position, that which affects us will ultimately affect the world.

Although you may feel, as many people do, that the animal rights movement does not affect you, that you can accept some of the ideology, but reject most, this "down to earth" look at the new phenomenon called "animal rights" will open your eyes to the fact that no American can continue to "sit on the fence" when it comes to this issue. Both sides are pulling you. The direction in which you decide to go could change the concept of moral behavior towards animals in America.

Every American owes it to himself, and to the animals that inhabit this world, to gain a better understanding of this new phenomenon called "animal rights."

CHAPTER 1
FOR THE LOVE OF ANIMALS?

The modern urban society is willing to share the life of their animals, but are unwilling to witness their deaths ... but death is a natural process of life.

The animal rights movement is promoted by its leaders as a natural and inevitable result of society's new awareness of animals, and why the present treatment of these innocent creatures should be recognized as unethical.

Most animal rights groups suggest that their primary goal is to educate society to the cruelties and exploitation of animals for what they describe as the petty and totally unnecessary needs of man.

Finally, animal rightists challenge people who profess a love for animals to demonstrate that love by attacking, and ultimately destroying, the present animal-use systems that survive through this cruel exploitation.

It is this declaration of love that stymies and confounds trappers, hunters and livestock farmers, in their attempts to understand the movement. They know that love can be shown in many different ways. How, when a person declares his or her love for animals as the reason for dedication to animal rights, can anyone argue against that declaration of love?

The more puzzling question they face, is how a society that has chosen to largely separate itself from animals, can condemn those who have chosen to make animals a large, and often necessary, part of their lives: people who demonstrate, often daily, their concerns not only for individual animals, but also for the preservation of whole species. I'm speaking, of course, about hunters, trappers and farmers.

A hunter does not hunt animals because he hates them, any more than a doctor chooses his profession because he hates humans. A farmer doesn't choose his profession because he hates cattle, any more than a veterinarian chooses his profession because he hates dogs and cats. A "vivisectionist" doesn't do research on animals because

12

he despises animals, but rather because he loves and cares for the human species.

Can the men and women who kill the tens of thousands of unwanted, dogs, cats, puppies and kittens, that are taken in by animals shelters each week be considered vicious and uncaring? Do they preform this service because they hate animals? THEY don't think so.

Our modern urban society has chosen to separate itself from daily life and death contact with animals, and is apparently satisfied to view them in the subservient role of pets, or in the detached world of television and literature. Most city dwellers find it impossible to understand that hunters, trappers and livestock farmers also love animals. But, because they have chosen to take an active part in both the life and DEATH of animals, and have developed a mutually beneficial relationship, such that the survival of one depends on the survival of both, this mutual dependency offends those who have separated themselves from the processes of nature.

A few years ago a local dairy farmer awoke in the middle of the night to find his barn engulfed in flames. In that barn were close to eighty cows that he had raised from calves. So attached had he become to these animals that he had even given them names. This was a herd of cattle which he had spent his whole life building, feeding and nurturing. In fact, he had spent more time with those cows that he had with his own children. Suddenly they were trapped in this burning inferno. Without hesitation, he picked up his rifle, and at great personal risk to his own life, entered the barn amid the hellish atmosphere of bellowing cattle, thick smoke and the roar of the burning inferno overhead, and walked down the rows of cattle and methodically put them out of their misery.

It is this beautiful act of mercy, that best illustrates the love that hunters, trappers and livestock farmers have for animals. They understand that for man to abandon animals, as this farmer could easily have done, is the true act of cruelty and abuse. Similarly, the hunter knows that if he doesn't pick up his rifle and thin his own herd, that it will ultimately suffer a greater degree of agony and despair as a result.

At the opposite extreme are professed animal lovers who support the animal rights groups. These are people who, if one of their pets were to become badly injured, could not face the responsibility of personally putting that animal out of its misery. If given the option of personally killing one pet to save several others, they can not force themselves to pull the trigger or insert the needle. So concerned are they for their own tender feelings that they hire veterinarians and animal shelters to do their dirty work for them. It takes great personal courage and strength to be a good shepherd of one's dependent creatures.

It is on this selfish protection of their own tender feelings, that the animal rights movement has grown. It is on this inability to face the harsh, and what appears to them, the cruelties of nature, that the animal rights movement flourishes today. It is a movement not built on love of animals, but rather on a love of self. Animal rights followers do not want to protect animals, they want to protect their own tender feelings.

A short time ago I received a harassment call from a woman from New Jersey. I listened for several minutes while she called me vicious, cruel and inhuman. I finally had the chance to ask her a question. I asked her; "Do you know that if it wasn't for the efforts of hunters and trappers, some animal species would be extinct?" Her answer confounded me, although I had heard it many times before. She returned; "Yes, but it's better for animals to become extinct, than to die at the hands of man."

It is this kind of mentality, that hunters and trappers confront every day, which they find difficult to understand. For too long, hunters and trappers have interpreted these statements as resulting from a lack of urban man's understanding of the role we play in the management of wildlife. Our urban citizens regard wildlife management as an example of cruelty to animals. They are no longer willing to condone or allow it, because man is responsible for animal deaths. Although nature may be more cruel in her dealing with creatures, urban man's separation from nature shields him from the natural world he would rather not face. Society as a whole does not have to face the reality of a starving herd of deer; few people see this. A slaughterhouse is a visual insult to their tender feelings, and a growing number of people want to end animal slaughter, so they won't have to bear the guilt.

Animal rights leaders have long understood that society has become hardened to the realities of humans butchering each other, great suffering and injustice, through our constant exposure to television, movies and literature. They recognize that urban separation from the realities of nature has made many people emotionally soft, and vulnerable to life and death matters that concern animals.

Animal rights groups have made very effective use of this fact, by constantly assaulting people's tender feelings through explicit visual advertising, and grotesque written descriptions of man's perceived inhumanities towards animals. The more innocent and vulnerable they can portray the animal, the more effective the campaign. In a very true sense they are using emotional blackmail to promote their cause, using a sense of personal guilt to encourage donations to each group.

Tenderness in love and feelings is too rare a part of the human spirit in these modern times to be abused and victimized in promoting a false cause. The greatest complaint I have against the animal rights movement is that it serves to turn these tender feelings into hate. It asks people to show their love for animals by cultivating hatred for hunters, trappers and farmers.

But, there is something more about the animal rights movement that rings hollow in the minds of the animal user groups. In all animal rights literature there are virtually no provisions that would truly allow for the survival of animals. Although they promise, in effect, to eliminate the visible assault on societies' tender feeling towards animals, they offer no alternate system that would provide for the care and nurturing of these objects of their declared love.

In view of this, it becomes apparent that the true goals of the animal rights leaders go far deeper than the simple profession of love for animals. After all, a man doesn't show his love for his family by deserting them when they need him most, when he is the only one who can save them. Animal rights leaders thoroughly understand the selfish motives of their followers.

In virtually all animal rights literature, there is absolutely no promise to totally eliminate animal suffering. They recognize that as long as there is life, there will be suffering, whether it is human or animal. What they do promise are higher moral and ethical standards for man. To accomplish this noble cause, in their eyes, the abandonment of our animals is a small price to pay. In effect, the animal rights movement is a selfish call for the betterment of man, at a great COST to animals.

People must understand that the animal rights ideology is in fact a form of ultra-modern religion that accepts people with varied degrees of faith, and with different motives. Although most people do not understand the true goals and doctrines of animal rights, even a small step in faith is recognized as a step in the "rights" direction. Although the call for love of animals is not a true goal of animal rights, it is good enough for the time being, because in the eyes of the leaders, a higher moral plane for man can only be achieved by hiding from the realities of nature.

It is no wonder that, with such goals in mind, the true believers recognize animal usage as petty and unnecessary. It is no wonder that they feel obliged to force their beliefs on others.

There are many supporters of the animal rights movement who truly do love animals, but in their efforts to show that love, they are allowing these moral and intellectual elitists to use that love in promotion of their own twisted and perverted ideology.

This animal rights doctrine actually sacrifices animals

for the moral advancement of man. It is an ideology written in Hell. Most people do not understand that this doctrine, which promises a higher moral evolution of man, has been presented, and more importantly rejected, countless times through thousands of years of history. The fact, that it is an idea that has taken root, and appears to be growing, at this point in history suggests that some very fundamental changes in society have occurred which allow this growth.

Society is being asked once again to accept or reject this age-old concept, and I won't deny you that decision. I only ask that you examine with me, all the parts of the puzzle; a puzzle with many complex, carefully-hidden, mysterious, often-denied parts that must be carefully put into place before the true picture of the animal rights ideology can be recognized.

CHAPTER 2
MAN--THE ULTIMATE PREDATOR

Because we never totally lost our instincts as hunters, or our taste for wild meat, we maintained our wild animal herds by continuing the role of predator. In so doing, we have placed upon ourselves a tremendous responsibility; the responsibility of maintaining and preserving the herds, both wild and domestic.

In a well publicized statement made by Ingrid Newkirk, founder of People for the Ethical Treatment Of Animals (PETA) she said; "A rat is a pig is a dog is a boy." This statement was taken by most to suggest that we are all animals, and because we have a comparable worth, each creature must be treated equal. Because hunters, trappers and farmers, more than most people recognize the value of animals, by their close association with animals they understand that the concept of equal worth and equal status is a perception that is foreign to nature. In fact, the natural laws and systems that govern nature PROVE Ms. Newkirk's statement to be fundamentally and biologically flawed.

Although her statement was a self-serving attempt to justify her own moral philosophy, with slight revisions, it is a statement that deserves more thought and evaluation.

If you put aside the moral implications of such statements, you are left with one fundamental question. If man is viewed simply as a higher form of mammal, than he must share common instincts and behavior with other mammals. To take this step in logic even farther, we must ask ourselves, by hint of our common nature and physiology, with what group of mammals can we most closely associate ourselves?

By refining Ms. Newkirk's statement slightly, a sound biological description could be formulated. By changing her statement to read; "A dog is a cat is a mink is a boy," a more accurate picture of the mammal, called man, is illustrated.

There are basically two types of mammals . . . predators

18

and their prey. There is virtually no living mammal, past or present, that doesn't fit into one of these two categories.

Although some predators may end up as a meal to a larger predator, their existence does not serve primarily as a source of food for other mammals. A polar bear will kill and eat a human, but he does not depend on humans as a source of food.

Predators hunt down, kill and feed on, prey species. They have eyes in the front of the head which enable them to better recognize and pursue their prey. Because of their relatively short digestive tracts they require meat, which is high in protein. Their teeth are designed to tear and chew flesh. Although all predators are classed as carnivores (meat eaters), like man the omnivore (food of all kinds) their diet must contain a percentage of roughage which they receive through hair, bones and feathers. For good health their diet must also contain substantial amounts of vegetation which they absorb in a partly digested form from the digestive tracts of smaller prey. No predator can survive by eating pure red meat. Predators are generally recognized to be the more intelligent of the mammalian species. This natural intelligence enables them to develop and refine hunting tactics which are necessary to find and pursue their prey. Finally, all predators are known for their natural aggression, and domination over, their prey.

On the opposite end of this biological scale are the prey species, animals which exist to provide food and protein for the predators. As would be expected, a very different biological profile can be drawn of the average prey creature. It has eyes at the sides of the head which enable it to see the approach of predators from all sides, including the rear. Prey species have longer digestive tracts which enable them to digest bulk forage. Their teeth are designed to grind and mince rough fiber. They are normally very prolific, and unless their numbers are controlled by predation, they soon over-populate and totally consume their food supply, resulting in massive die-offs. With few exceptions, most prey species are well down the mammalian list in regard to intelligence, and their actions and reactions are more the result of instincts than a recognizable thought process. In a panic situation, whole flocks of sheep have been known to follow their leader over a cliff to their deaths, and we have all heard of the mass drowning of lemmings when their migrations reach the sea.

When a direct comparison is made between man, and both predatory and prey species, it becomes very obvious that man is through common physical characteristics A PREDATOR. Thus the statement "A dog is a cat is a mink is a boy." All predators.

Not only does man fit most of the physical criteria needed to be classified as predators, more importantly, the mere fact that humans have the "hunter" instinct, an instinct that we share with no other animal of the prey species, suggest that we are also predators by NATURE.

When man is viewed in this light, many dark and foreboding implications come to mind. At this point, the moral implications of this possibility must be faced. Do our predatory instincts explain man's inhumanities to man? Do they imply that man has a basically vicious nature that can only be changed by evolution? Or is it an excuse for man to dominate his environment, and other mammals, birds and fish in that environment?

If we truly have evolved into predators, and dislike the idea, it's only natural to attempt to change that reality. The first, and most obvious step would be to become vegetarians. By so doing, we would start the evolutionary process which would ultimately eliminate our aggressive and dominant nature. The second step would be to become totally self-centered in our position in nature in relation to other animals. All species, including man, would be totally on their own. Survival or extinction would be ultimately determined by the laws of nature. Laws that we would break by virtue of our decision, as I will soon explain.

By design, it is obvious that this unguided direction is where the animal rights ideology would take us. The basic animal rights ideology dictates that because of our moral and intellectual superiority, we have no other choice.

It is obvious that the animal rights movement is in existence to force a change in our present evolutionary position in nature. It is apparently their intent to change us from aggressive wolves into docile sheep; dominant lions into subservient cattle; and thus eliminate what they also view as the vicious and barbaric behavior of man.

The basic flaw in this doctrine is that it promotes a mixed message. On one hand, it leaves the ultimate fate of all animals to the laws of nature. On the other hand it denies the basic character of man which was shaped by nature, thus placing in question the ultimate wisdom of nature.

By denying that we are born predators, and taking steps to change our basic nature for moral and intellectual reasons, the animal rights ideology condemns nature itself. At the same time they throw on the mercy of this flawed nature, the future of all animal species.

Those who wish to remain full participants in the natural processes of life and death on this earth accept the idea that we are predators, and live with the ramifications such a classification would imply. In so doing, we must face the reality of being the ultimate predator, and must decide the moral implications of such a high position in nature.

If we decide that man is nothing more than another animal, created through evolution, as Ms. Newkirk's statement implies, then we must live by the laws of the nature that created us. To do otherwise would be a form of rebellion against our own evolution.

Fortunately, we are not on the same level as the rat, the pig and the dog. No other animal in nature has morals or compassion. A fox would not consider the moral consequences of eating the last rabbit. The cat does not have compassion for the mouse, nor does the coyote have compassion for the deer. Such emotions would actually be dangerous to the survival of these animals.

The only creature on earth which displays morals and

compassion is man. They are two, among many differences that separate us from animals. The question is, can we deny or accept our predatory instincts totally on the basis of morals?

To answer this we must look to nature for an example. The mountain lion and the deer are good examples of two species that interact with each other. The mountain lion depends on the deer as a source of food. At the same time, the health of the deer herd depends on the mountain lion to weed out the sickly members. This is important not only to eliminate genetically inferior animals, but also to prevent the spread of disease that sick animals may transmit to the rest of the herd. The mountain lion also helps to regulate the herd numbers, preventing the herd from reaching populations which might over-stress the food supplies, resulting in mass starvation.

Because the mountain lion was not compatible with man, it has been eliminated from much of its range, and man has replaced the cat as predator. Many people condemn this intrusion on nature, but there are numerous examples in nature of one predator replacing another. The replacement of "man the predator" with "mountain lion the predator" is not an insult against nature.

The true insult against nature is when the predator is eliminated, and not replaced. In so doing, one link in a long chain is broken. At that point, the prey herd becomes endangered. Without a predator to control their numbers the herd expands to the point where stress is placed on it, at which time the animals start dying from disease and starvation. Soon the herd is eliminated. Another link is broken. Subsequently other predators which depend on the herd are eradicated. Another link is broken. When the herd destroys the food supply, they eliminate the food and shelter for other animals. Another link is broken. Soon, the chain of life becomes a chain of death.

The final questions we must ask ourselves are; 1. Is it morally right for us to abandon our position as predator? 2. What kind of death and destruction will result from this fundamental separation from our place in nature?

3. How, after all these thousands of years, could we decide to abandon the herd?

The first question can only be answered by addressing the implications presented by the last two. There are a few people in our society who, by virtue of their position in life, feel oppressed. Still others feel great compassion for other oppressed creatures. The more helpless and innocent other creatures appear, the greater the feelings of anger such people feel, against those who, in their view, are the oppressors.

To these people, the docile cow, the innocent lamb, the timid deer, are objects of pity. In their eyes, any exploitation of these animals translates into one word ... abuse.

The problem with this philosophy is that it does not explain the mountain lion's right to exploit the deer. This is, of course, explained anyway by the simple proclamation that man no longer needs to kill the deer. He can easily become a vegetarian, a choice the mountain lion cannot make. Although this provides the basis for this animal rights doctrine, it doesn't answer the most important question; what happens if we do abandon our natural position as predator?

To explain this final question, we must first understand why we are the ultimate predator. At some time in our distant past, our ancestors made an important decision. That decision has shaped our history over thousands of years. That decision was to abandon the life of the nomadic hunter, and become shepherds of the herd. Our favorite prey species were captured and tamed. To help us manage the herd, we made use of another predator, the dog, to help us control and protect the herd.

This decision suddenly enabled us to build permanent homes, villages and cities. It made it possible for us to build and share our knowledge, grow crops and mature into the civilized societies we are today. Those cultures who never made this transformation, the Eskimos, some American Indians, and the Bushmen of Australia, are destined to face increasing challenges in a changing world that doesn't value their cultures. As our populations

23

grew, and our herd become larger, we found it necessary to eliminate, right or wrong, other predators that invaded our territory. In so doing, we either killed off those predators, or pushed them back into areas unsuitable for farming. We thus eliminated the threat from mountain lions, wolves and grizzly bears.

Because we never totally lost our instincts as hunters, or our taste for wild meat, we maintained our wild animal herds by continuing the role of predator. In so doing, we have placed upon ourselves a tremendous responsibility, the responsibility of maintaining and preserving all herds, both wild and domestic.

Slowly but surely, we secured a dominant position as the ultimate predator.

The abandonment of that predatory responsibility, would mean the virtual extinction of countless animal species. Without the care and feeding of our cattle, pigs, sheep, chickens, turkeys and horses they would soon perish, with only a few left to serve as oddities in special preserves. In fact, this is what the animal rights groups suggest must happen. Such creatures should be "managed" without being USED by man.

Without natural predators, our deer, elk and moose would soon become pests that would destroy our crops and damage our woodlands. In an effort to protect our crops these animals would be trapped, shot, poisoned or purposely infected with deadly communicable diseases, and their carcasses discarded. Ultimately they would over-populate, and die off in massive numbers. As I have illustrated previously, this destruction of natural feed supplies would have an appalling effect on other forms of animal life which depend on the same food supplies. Whether urban people believe it or not, this has happened time and again.

If the animal rights movement eliminates the fur industry, equal devastation would result. Beaver populations will increase dramatically, causing great damage by flooding valuable woodlands, flooding roads and plugging drain pipes. They would destroy valuable ornamental trees and fruit trees. Raccoons can also increase to tremendous numbers, and as long as there are farmers' crops in the fields for them to feed on, their populations will grow until they are destroyed by poison, or by diseases such as distemper and rabies. Likewise, muskrats are very prolific animals and can soon literally eat themselves out of house and home, destroying valuable marsh lands which are critical to the survival of some of ou most endangered species. In the absence of the fur trad drastic measures will have to be taken to control th numbers. Coyotes are also increasing in numbers across the U.S. and are invading areas of the East wh they were seldom found before. Without controls b exerted on their numbers, through trapping, they ar creasingly destructive to farmers' livestock, and in s conditions can become a danger to pets and man him

At present, very effective controls are being exer trappers, but with the passing of the fur industry animals will no longer have a monetary value, an controls will be eliminated. In the absence of a f ket, these animals would still have to be killed, their carcasses would be burned or thrown into a buried. This waste and suffering from disease an is considered an unnecessary and tragic sin by t animal users.

Although many people will refuse to believe happen, it must be understood that numerou constantly being introduced at both the state level which, if passed into law, would virtual the harvest of these animals. The animal r are very serious in their intent to totally e harvest of all wild creatures.

Virtually every animal rights leader pro vegetarian, thus showing the ultimate goa ment. That goal is, of course, a vegetarian s more willing to accept such an eventua other Americans, but the reality is, they close. By unwittingly supporting major re raising of livestock, Americans can plac on farmers. By destroying the veal market, the animal rights movement would destroy a very important part of the dairy farmers' income. By requiring more spacious housing for all forms of livestock, the cost of raising stock would rise dramatically. Even a relatively small rise in the price of chicken, beef and pork, eliminates its availability to tens of thousands of low income households. As the price increases, still more homes will have to go without, until only a small proportion of Americans can afford what would soon be a luxury. In effect, a large proportion of American households would be forced into a vegetarian lifestyle.

Again, if you think this is a little too far fetched to believe, look at many of the Eastern European, and third world countries. In Romania for example, one of the biggest complaints from the people after they recently forced their independence from the Communist system, was that they had been forced to survive with virtually no meat. In many of these countries, because of the high cost of meat, they had become virtual vegetarians, while the leaders of the nation had plentiful supplies of meat.

Over the last several years there has been a virtual avalanche of bills introduced at the state and national level, through the direct efforts of animal rights groups, that would greatly hamper the farmers' ability to produce low price, and affordable meat and dairy products. With each new year the pressure on lawmakers to implement these bills grows at an accelerating rate.

The alleged intent of these bills is to improve animal welfare, but their real goal is "to cut down, and finally eliminate all animal use." (PETA)

CHAPTER 3
ANIMAL RIGHTS...THE ILLUSIONS

At present we have an abundance of livestock, and our woods hold a greater supply of wildlife than at any time in our history, and at no time in our history have we appreciated them less. In view of this aberration in human nature, it obviously follows that once man no longer feels a need for animals, he develops a moral ideology which justifies their abandonment.

The basic worldwide philosophy concerning the relationship between man and animals has been long established on the concept that man had dominion over all animals. This philosophy was universally accepted almost from the beginning of man's history.

The prehistoric hunter, in order to be successful, had to develop a very extensive understanding of his prey. Although it is reasonable to assume that animals were very plentiful at that time in history, man's weapons were very crude, making his job of bringing down his prey very difficult and dangerous. It was often necessary for the hunter to risk his life to feed his family.

As the human population grew, and man's weapons became more sophisticated, the prey species became less plentiful and his knowledge of the animals' nature, habits and methods of evasion became even more important. Man's skill as a hunter was so important to these ancient peoples, that the most skillful hunters were shown great respect by other members of the group, and were often chosen as leaders by virtue of their courage and skill.

More importantly, the wealth of each group was measured by the abundance of animals in its territory. It's reasonable to assume that the first provocation of war resulted from protection of these hunting grounds from competing or invading bands or tribes. It simply follows that those which held the greatest wealth, also faced the greatest threat of losing that wealth to the less fortunate. Unless the wealthy group became outnumbered to the point at which they were overwhelmed by outsiders, their wealth usually enabled them to dominate for a time.

Throughout history it was the poorer nations or tribes

which played the most important part in the evolution of society. Wealthy tribes and nations invariably set their sights on frivolous things. They became wasteful with their wealth until ultimately their wealth ran out.

Through necessity, poorer nations become more resourceful, inventive and frugal with their more meager resources. It is through necessity rather than wealth that society is raised to a higher level.

It's safe to assume that those early bands of hunters and gatherers, who were wealthy in terms of wildlife, found no provocation to cultivate the soil. For them there was no need. History shows that the less wealthy tribes were the first to start domesticating animals, and till the soil. In so doing, they dramatically diminished the wealth of the hunters' prey. They literally developed something that was more valuable than wild animals. Because of the greater value of domestic animals and farmlands, the first step in the rejection of all animals was put into place.

But, for a time, man came to rely on domestic animals more and more for food, transportation and a source of brute power to cultivate his crops. This reliance could almost be looked upon as a partnership between man and beast. The survival of both often hinged on the survival of one. It could be argued very forcefully, that without the help of animals, humans could not have advanced to the level of sophistication present today. That sophistication is illustrated not only in man's lifestyle, but also in his physical advancement. In cultures where meat has long been a part of the diet, people are generally larger in stature, while people who live largely on fruits and grains are usually physically smaller.

Through the act of clearing land to produce valuable crops, men destroyed the habitat of many wild animals. Although they tolerated the presence of some wild animals, other animals that were viewed as a threat to their new wealth were soon eliminated or pushed back into areas unsuitable for farming.

Although man's understanding of wildlife has never been totally lost, it eventually became more important to develop a better understanding of domestic animals. From this need came modern veterinary medicine and husbandry sciences which helped man nurture and maintain the herds.

It may be hard for modern man to understand that it wasn't simply land that these people valued. If that were true, mountain land would have been as valuable as bottom land. The true value of a farmer's land is not determined by its volume, but rather its fertility and how much grain and meat it will produce. Because good land was, and is, in short supply, it has always been valuable.

But, as history has shown, man's perception of true riches quickly changes. As I have already indicated, as societies become richer they become more frivolous in their view of riches. The great Roman Empire ultimately fell as a result of the importance they placed on frivolous things. Things that did not truly add to man's existence, or work to preserve that existence. Instead they turned their energies to entertainment and luxury. They left as their legacy great works of art, and the ruins of their once opulent cities.

As a society, they became a product of human nature, a part of human nature that in spite of all the wisdom and enlightenment we have supposedly achieved over the generations, has not even minutely changed. It could even be argued that over time our perception of what is truly valuable to the survival and preservation of man's existence has diminished to a pitiful low. As a species, we have in many ways become less aware of our true riches than the ancient hunter, who at least recognized the importance of animals to his survival.

In modern man's personal search for material riches and luxury, he has diminished the value of his greatest treasures; his land, air and water.

Only after these great treasures became tarnished has man started to again recognize their great value. But these are not the only treasures we continue to squander. For the modern riches of a career, entertainment and personal gratification we have started to squander our greatest earthly treasure . . . our children. To enrich our short stay here on earth we are trading our spiritual riches to satisfy our lust for wine, women and song . . . and now drugs.

Man has one dominant flaw in his character. He values something only if it's in short supply. Gold is a good example. The moment there is even a slight hint of an increased production of gold, the price drops on world markets. An even better example of our disdain for abundance, can be illustrated by the abuse of our land, air and water. Because these life sustaining resources appeared to be unlimited and free, we treated them with utter disdain. We held them in such low regard that we filled them with our waste.

At present we have an abundance of livestock, and our woods hold a greater supply of wildlife than at any time in our history, and at no time in history have we appreciated them less. In view of this aberration in human nature, it obviously follows that once man no longer feels a need for animals, he develops a moral ideology which justifies their abandonment.

All of this illustrates man's self-serving and destructive nature. That nature is guided by a personal moral philosophy that often changes in words, but seldom in intent. It is an ever changing philosophy that invariably destroys the value of man's ancient treasures, and replaces them with worthless trinkets. Man's selfish nature is no better illustrated than in his desire to turn his face from nature, and hide from what modern man perceives as the brutal realities of nature. So powerful is this need to protect our tender feelings, that we have started to replace reality with illusions.

Today, modern urban societies still value animals, but now they take the form of soft cuddly stuffed toys, cartoon characters and puppets. Gone is the pain and suffering inherent to nature. Suddenly animals have "super human" and "God-like" qualities. They have the ability to communicate with man, to walk on air, never age, and can survive great injury without blemish. They are born without sin, and have life eternal.

Although animal rights leaders mock people for the display of vanity which they feel is illustrated in their desire to wear fur coats, that same level of society staged a massive ceremony that was covered by television networks and major publications that celebrated the birthday of A MOUSE!

The frivolity of all this is best illustrated by the fact that if modern man presents animals in the form of an illusion, society will make him rich and famous; if he presents them in reality he is scorned and ridiculed.

This illusion can only be complete when every trace of reality is erased from man's presence. It only follows that the next step is to turn our leather shoes and beautiful furs into plastic. Turn from the natural warmth of wool garments to clothing made from chemicals.

Even our pets have become a part of the illusion. They are accepted into this "make believe" world only if they conform to the fantasy. They must become subservient; like the "perfect" child. They must be good enough at mimicking human behavior to be viewed, and described, as "almost" human. Finally, they must "give up" their vicious predatory behavior in our presence.

This illusion, which is enforced by the animal rights movement, not only represents the ideology of animal rights . . . IT IS ANIMAL RIGHTS.

The modern animal rights movement was thus spawned from the "make believe" world which now provides its greatest support and encouragement. The fantasy world of lions without courage, little green frogs that talk and big yellow birds.

CHAPTER 4
RETURNING ANIMALS TO NATURE

Although the animal rights ideology calls for the return of all animals to the care of nature, the time has long since passed that nature has held the power to shepherd the herds.

Vermont born George Perkins Marsh once said; "Man is everywhere a disturbing agent. Wherever he plants his feet, the harmonies of nature are turned to discords. The proportions and accommodations which insure the stability of existing arrangements are overthrown." (1)

One does not have to enter into a long dissertation to explain how man has changed the face of nature. One only has to travel the length of the New Jersey turnpike from Delaware to New York to see, and even smell man's handiwork. Even a short drive through the lush farmlands of southeastern Pennsylvania illustrates the changes man has wrought on the original intent of nature.

What many people don't understand is that by changing the face of nature man has displaced many of its original inhabitants. By destroying the great unbroken woodlands of the east to produce farmland, man destroyed the habitat for the elk, the wolf and the mountain lion. These, and other species of animals could no longer survive and flourish in this altered environment Although other, more adaptable animals, have filled in this new environment, nature's system of checks and balances was forever altered. Even more apparent was the change in the ratio of predator and prey species. Although the deer replaced the elk in this new habitat, there was no suitable replacement for the wolf and mountain lion which regulated the herd. By virtue of man's presence in this new environment, the larger predators were pushed to more remote areas.

By the virtual existence of man, the face of nature, its laws and its systems are not only disrupted, but in large part, destroyed.

By destroying the feeding and breeding grounds of the

passenger pigeon, man broke up the flocks and doomed the whole species to extinction. By destroying the habitat of the mountain lion and the wolf, man pushed them back to the farthest corner of the wilderness where their survival hangs by a thread.

Although it is possible, and in fact may be imperative, to heal some of the scars we have caused to nature, it can never return to its original form. Man has forever defaced nature and altered and replaced its systems with systems of his own.

As the populations of man grows he gobbles up huge tracts of land that animals call home. With every passing day, man paves over 2,000 acres of land which are lost forever to wildlife; 1,500 acres of marshlands are drained and filled; thousands of acres of forests are slashed and cut.

With an increasing number of people moving to more rural areas, and building homes and cottages, more and more wildlife habitat is being devoured. Every time a structure is built in a rural setting, valuable habitat is being destroyed forever. Unfortunately, most people choose to build their homes in the very best wildlife nesting, breeding and feeding grounds.

This loss of habitat has had a very negative effect on many wildlife species that can only escalate in the future. As the wild animals' feeding and nesting grounds continue to decrease they are forced to occupy smaller areas, causing increased crowding and competition for feed and cover. Without the careful management of these herds even more habitat will be destroyed by the animals themselves, through overfeeding and physical destruction of habitat. Because these areas are usually occupied by a variety of different animal species, an overpopulation of one animal species can also cause damage to the habitat of other resident species. Overpopulation of muskrats in the Louisiana tidal marshes for example, have been proven to produce "eat outs" which destroys the marsh habitat not only for many future generations of muskrats, but also for many marsh birds and waterfowl. Overpopulation of deer in a woodland setting can gobble up feed supplies for rabbits, turkeys and squirrels.

An even greater danger presented by this overcrowding, is the potential spread of disease that comes with close contact between animals, which has the potential of destroying whole populations of wildlife.

Theodore Roosevelt, although not the first to recognize this destruction being wrought on nature, was at least the first to try to do something about it, and started the National Park System. As a devoted hunter and sportsman, he started the modern conservation system that has been kept alive by other dedicated sportsmen ever since.

Although the animal rights ideology calls for the return of all animals to the care of nature, the time is long since passed that nature has held the power to shepherd the herds. It is not only unrealistic, but naive, to expect nature to immediately heal the wounds, and restore its laws, after man has so long ignored and altered them.

To survive, all animals must be cared for by man, and our system of shepherds and herds is best suited to do that job.

Man wants to commit back to nature, and the care of nature, all of earth's animals, while at the same time, he is unwilling and unable to return to nature himself. Because this cannot happen, nature is forever crippled in its ability to shepherd its own herds.

CHAPTER 5
SHEPHERDS OF THE HERDS AND FLOCKS

For his hard work, toil and dedicated service, the shepherd receives nourishment from his herd by harvesting the excess. By harvesting only that portion of the herd that is not needed, or that would die anyway, the shepherd keeps his herd strong.

There is a unique quality in the human spirit that may be the cornerstone on which man has built his dominant position in nature.

All of nature is built on a system that can be broken down into two basic categories; the shepherd and the flock. The mountain lion and the wolf are both shepherds of their flocks, put there by nature. Although man is also a shepherd, by the strength or weakness of his spirit, he is the only creature who has the choice of becoming a good shepherd or a bad shepherd. Or worse still, he may totally abandon his responsibility as shepherd, and abandon his flocks.

All of mankind can be recognized as a flock, but throughout this huge flock are found many shepherds. The leader of a nation is a shepherd over his people; parents are the shepherds of their family flock; the Red Cross is a shepherd of the needy; and generals are shepherds over their army.

Like animals, we are all members of the flock, but unlike animals, we are all shepherds of the flock to the degree which we recognize and accept that responsibility. We each have the power to be good shepherds, and are limited only by the strength and quality of our spirit, and our willingness to prepare ourselves for the burden. There are countless examples of people, who by the strength of their spirit, have become good shepherds; like Washington who led his flock to greatness; like Eisenhower who led his flock to victory. There are shepherds who nurture and feed their family flock, and who help the sick, the helpless and the homeless.

It is only when man abandons his position as a good shepherd that the ugly side of human nature begins to show. When a leader of a nation forgets the welfare of the flock, the nation begins to crumble. When a general directs his flock wrongly, it leads to defeat. When a shepherd harvests too much wealth from his human flock, it starts to suffer the misery of poverty, disease and neglect.

This system of shepherds and flocks is important to the well-being of the human family, and it is the interaction of a large number of these systems that has allowed humankind to flourish.

These same principles also apply to the interaction between man and animal. Over the centuries, man has become shepherds of many herds. The trapper shepherds one herd, the hunter another and the farmer still another. The trappers' herd is made up of all the furbearing animals, the hunters' herd is the game animals and the farmers' herd is the domestic animals.

Each of these shepherd groups has set up systems to manage these herds. The trappers and hunters hire game protectors to manage and enforce the harvest of the herd. They pay biologists to study the herd so it can be managed properly, and they restock, feed and nurture the herds.

The farmer has broken up his herds into smaller numbers and each farmer shepherds his own small herd with the help of veterinarians, animal nutritionists, etc. For his hard work, toil and dedicated service the shepherd receives nourishment from his herd, by harvesting the excess. By harvesting only that portion of the herd that is not needed, or that would die anyway, the shepherd keeps his herd strong.

"I am wont to think that men are not so much the keepers of herds as herds are keepers of men, the former are so much freer."

Henry David Thoreau.

Just as mankind flourishes through the interaction of many such systems, the interaction of the animal herds and their shepherds is critical to their collective survival.

It is each shepherd's job to be sure that his herd doesn't interfere or harm the other herds. The trapper manages the coyote population so that they don't destroy the hunters' game or the farmers' livestock. He manages the muskrats so they don't destroy the habitat of game, or destroy livestock ponds. The hunter controls the game so they don't destroy the farmers' crops and spread disease to his livestock. The farmer provides food and habitat for both game and furbearers.

Like the original systems set into place by nature, it is an interdependent network of systems that enhance each other. This concept of interacting systems suggests that the humans who built this system understood nature intimately as it is a very close imitation of the original intent of nature.

Although animal rights advocates suggest that this system is morally corrupt, for man to turn his back on the herds at this time in history would devastate these delicate systems. To abandon even one herd would eliminate all management, and controls on that herd, as well as disrupt the interdependent systems between herds, which would allow the introduction of disease, starvation and neglect.

The leaders of many different nations have been willing to allow that to happen to their flocks, but the shepherds of the animal herds care too much for their wards to commit them back to the flawed hands of nature.

CHAPTER 6
DESTROYING THE OLD SYSTEMS

There is little doubt that animal rights leaders feel that although "animal liberation" is historically inevitable, it must be guided by a well-disciplined core of "professional revolutionaries." It is an ideology taken from the political and economic principles of Leninism, and followed to the letter by the animal rights leaders.

The concept of animal liberation has a very long history. In early Greek history the philosopher Pythagoras was a vegetarian who encouraged respect for animals for what was apparently his religious belief that animals housed the spirits of dead humans. Fortunately, the wisdom of Aristotle and other philosophers through history prevailed, and except for the Hindu and some small cult religions, man placed no religious value on animals.

Over the intervening years small fringe groups, and solitary individuals, kept the idea of animal liberation alive, but it was an idea considered too radical to gain much strength at a time when many people were still chopping the heads off chickens, and cleaning them for Sunday dinner.

Until shortly after World War II, it was very common for families, even in medium size cities, to produce their own meat, eggs and dairy products. Those who didn't raise their own animals could usually buy them from someone in the neighborhood. In fact, many chickens were shipped live to the inner city, where they were butchered and cleaned just prior to sale. Most chickens, ducks, geese and smaller animals were usually butchered just prior to eating them, and often by the lady of the house. Large animals were usually butchered late in the fall so the cooler weather would keep the meat fresh until it was smoked, canned or salted for preservation.

All this was necessary because of poor storage facilities. Even after World War II, many people in rural areas of the U.S. were still using ice boxes which utilized large chunks of ice, cut and stored during the winter, to cool their milk and other groceries during the heat of summer.

But times were changing. After World War II, farming practices become more specialized and efficient. It was through this specialized farming that farmers were able to produce chickens, eggs, meats and dairy products so efficiently that high quality farm products became more costly to raise on a small scale than they were to buy at the local grocery store. Through the use of better refrigeration units, transportation and storage of farm products became easier, eliminating the need to butcher livestock just prior to eating, or to preserve meats with salt and smoke.

For thousands of years, man raised cattle and hogs to eat, and gave little thought to their slaughter. After cleaning their dung, working hard in the hot fields to harvest their feed, feeding them morning and night and putting up with their often stubborn behavior, it was never hard to butcher them. After all, that was what they were raised for, and most people were thankful for their blessings.

But, with surprising quickness, the close association between man and his livestock was to end. Within one generation, the separation by a huge majority of society was complete. By the mid 60's, most young people at high school or college age, knew virtually nothing about livestock. In fact, if asked where their meat come from, they would reply with perfect innocence, that it came from the local supermarket. The time was ripe for the re-emergence of the old concept of animal liberation.

In the early 1970's, Peter Singer, recognized by many as the guru of animal rights, at the tender age of twenty nine wrote his book "Animal Liberation," which is recognized today as the "Bible" of the animal rights movement. In reality, it was simply an expanded version of a book titled "Animals' Rights" by Henry S. Salt, written close to a century earlier.

Even earlier in his career, Mr. Singer authored another book titled "Democracy and Disobedience" in which he deliberated on the value of disobedience and revolt in a Democratic system.

No other person in the animal rights movement better

exemplifies the ideology represented by the movement than Mr. Singer. Born in Melbourne, Australia, in 1946 and educated at the University of Melbourne and at Oxford during the campus rebellion of the 60's, he is obviously a product of the counterculture spawned from that era.

At no time in American history were the radicals and dissenters within our society given a greater voice than during the mid 60's. It was a time when the call to change our democratic system was at its loudest. With the end of the Vietnam War, the call for revolution soon faded for lack of good justification, and most of its participants faded into society. But, in the hearts of many, the seeds of revolution had become too deeply rooted. It was from these roots of rebellion against the system, any system, that the modern version of animal liberation, known today as animal rights, was truly re-born.

Without the Vietnam War as a rationale for change, it follows that this small band of intellectual and moral elitists had to find another cause on which to force its will. In the natural progression of things, it follows that through the simple power of their intellects, this small band championed the ideology of animal liberation. Because it is viewed as an ideology which has the power to change the world and its age old systems, it was embraced with enthusiasm; not only by many of the elitists of our society, but also the extremists, as exemplified by the Charles Manson cult. It comes very close to being the ultimate form of rebellion against a system.

It comes as no surprise that the democratic system Mr. Singer wrote about in his book "Democracy and Disobedience" was not the same system of management set up within the animal rights organizations. It is also no surprise that the tactics used to force change in our system, are frowned upon in this democracy.

There is little doubt that animal rights leaders feel that although "Animal Liberation" is historically inevitable, it must be guided by a well-disciplined core of "professional revolutionaries." It is an ideology taken from the political and economic principles of Leninism, and followed to the letter by the animal rights leaders.

It is also apparent that this small group of leaders recognize themselves as so morally and intellectually superior that they can ignore the age-old philosophy that says man has dominion over animals. They know that they can force change through the strategy that "the end will justify the means."

In view of this, it is not unreasonable to assume that animal rights has been patterned after Communism, in both spirit and substance. Although I would hesitate to call the leaders of the movement Communists, and can see no benefit in doing so, it is very apparent that they are students of the Marxist/Leninist's system of human manipulation.

Although hunters, trappers and farmers lament the sudden growth of the animal rights movement, it's just possible that we may ultimately be thankful that this small group of rebels chose animal liberation as their cause.

First of all, the animal rights movement is a call to free creatures which are "oppressed" by our present system. It calls for the rich and influential of our society to provide a "voice" for these oppressed creatures. The "voice" is, of course, that of the animal rights groups.

Secondly, it is a movement that is led by a very small core of leaders; less than 100 people. Although these groups claim memberships totaling well into the millions, all policies and objectives are dictated by this small band of professionals. Members do not have a vote in even low level decisions, or even to change their leadership. "Members are actually paid-up supporters."

Third, the movement is basically an atheistic movement that openly condemns the Judeo-Christian ethic concerning animals. Animal rights believers have no tolerance for any established religions with the possible exception of the Hindu, because of its worship of cattle.

Fourth, the animal rights ideology calls for the "oppressed" segments of our society, the minorities and women to "rise up" for "the cause" of animal rights. In fact, for a number of years the movement was known as "animal liberation," which closely resembled the Communist call for liberation of the masses. But, with the corresponding growth of civil rights and woman's rights, it was quickly decided that re-adoption of the term "animal rights" would gain more acceptance. After all, how could whole segments of society, who were fighting so desperately for their human rights, deny those same rights to animals? It was a well calculated move, and almost immediately the movement gained more impetus.

Fifth, it is a movement that openly justifies terrorism as a means of changing "the system."

Finally, it manipulates the public through the careful use of propaganda that stirs the emotions, often to irrational levels of passion.

But, as the recent events in eastern Europe have proven, the Communist system is a big lie. While it promises relief for the oppressed, in reality, it oppresses them even more; it is a system that decreases the value of human life, and can only flourish in the shadows of ignorance; it replaces traditional religious faith with a new ideology, and can only survive through subterfuge and intimidation. Ultimately, it is a process that is designed to destroy a system, but is incapable of building a new and better one in its place.

When you consider the fact that there are 20 million hunters and trappers, 3 million farmers, and tens of millions of people who draw their livelihood from these industries, as opposed to possibly 100 thousand hard core animal rights activists, it becomes obvious that the real power of the animal rights movement is a sham.

But, through the clever manipulation of our system of government, a small group of dedicated leaders, and their small band of intellectual elitists, have built an illusion of power that goes far beyond the bounds of reality.

They have accomplished this, first by offering a many-faceted ideology, in which the acceptance of one idea makes you a part of the whole. By rejecting the use of animals for research, a person will often describe himself as a supporter of animal rights, although he continues eating meat. Few people realize that by accepting and supporting one aspect of the ideology, they produce support and power for the total concept of animal rights. Anti-vivisection, anti-fur, vegetarianism, anti-hunting, etc., all come under the blanket heading of "animal rights." If you support one part of the movement, you support it all.

By attacking on numerous different fronts, the animal rights industry negates the awesome power of the opposition. The animal rights movement is a guerrilla attack that separates its opposition by many different skirmishes while it operates under one banner; "animal rights." As in any guerrilla war, where the power of the opposition is so overpowering, it will be a long, and very likely, a bloody battle. In fact, animal rights leaders are constantly telling their followers that it will be years before they reach their ultimate goals.

It is also obvious that some of these groups are preparing themselves for a protracted struggle. The animal rights group Fund for Animals for example has invested heavily in the stock market. According to their public inspection tax form in 1985, they purchased over a half million dollars worth of stock in 1984. Investments were made in Mobil Oil, Petroleum Invis Ltv, Valero Energy Corp, Diamond Shamrock and others.

The final step in any guerrilla war requires the ultimate face to face, power against power, showdown between the opposing forces. To win this final battle, the animal rights guerrillas must work diligently to destroy the power and influence of the opposing forces.

It is in this slow, but very progressive erosion of the power and influence now held by hunters, trappers, livestock farmers and research institutions that the animal rights guerrillas are most effective.

In their efforts to destroy the power of the opposition, they are using very predictable methods, proven successful in many parts of the world.

The first is to divide and conquer. Once divided, concentrate your attack on the weakest link, which is at this time, of course, the trapping industry.

By attacking all shepherd/herd groups simultaneously, each group sets up defenses designed to protect itself first. The threat is perceived as coming from different sources, different enemies, resulting in division. At first, the guerrillas will only use harassment techniques to keep the stronger forces busy while they concentrate their greatest energies on what they recognize is the weakest link in the defenses. In this case the trapper, followed closely by fur farmers, the bow hunter, the dog hunters, etc. This is a clear example of the domino theory put into practice. The death of an army starts with the death of one.

The second step being followed is labeling of the opposition as cruel destroyers of oppressed creatures, with greed as their only motive. In addition, the animal rights movement labels the activities of animal users as unnecessary and fruitless.

Through the use of gruesome pictures, stolen video tapes and endless propaganda, the animal right groups have been very successful at recruiting Americans into supporting at least one, and often several, of their causes. Today it would be very hard, even among our own ranks, to find someone who didn't oppose the portrayed "cruelty and greed" represented by one of our industries. It would not be hard today to find a hunter or doctor who hasn't become a victim of the animal rights propaganda, and who thinks trapping was cruel. Or, possibly a hunter or trapper who thought animal research was cruel.

More importantly, through their use of propaganda, the animal rights guerrillas have labeled furs, hunting, the raising of veal and medical research on animals as totally unnecessary, providing no benefits to society, or to the animals themselves. Each industry is portrayed as existing to satisfy the greed and selfishness of the oppressors.

The third step is to destroy their lifelines and hamper their activities.

The most obvious example of this is the effort to destroy the glamour and elegance represented by fur. They make fur buyers guilty of the "sins" of the trapper and mink rancher, thus hoping to destroy our lifeline. But, more subtle is the effort to place restrictions on hunters, farmers and medical labs. By placing restrictions on these groups, they weaken their strength and resolve.

The fourth step is to use the opposition's own power against them. Our greatest strength is our system of government that provides representatives for each segment of society. By going to urban politicians the animal rights guerrillas are able to promote legislation that would restrict the activities of the animal user groups, and thus place great burdens on their systems. This manipulation of urban politicians is apparently very easy considering the fact that urban politicians don't have trappers, farmers and hunters as their constituents.

The final step is to infiltrate your enemies' own institutions. Work from within as well as from outside to disable them.

The animal rights efforts to influence CITES makes it very apparent that they wish to pervert those institutions that were created by those of us who feel it is important to police our own ranks. If the animal rights guerrillas can become our policemen, they will destroy us.

Ultimately it must be understood by the American people that the animal rights movement is not a struggle for fame or fortune. It is a struggle for POWER.

By destroying the shepherd/herd systems a power vacuum will be created, which only the animal rights groups will be in position to fill.

The most frightening aspect of such an eventuality is that once they achieve this power, they will use it to force the abandonment of the herds.

Trans-Species Unlimited, a national organization based in Pennsylvania, simply observes that "the animal rights movement is a power struggle, a societal conflict between oppressors and oppressed" . . . "a struggle for the total liberation of planet Earth and its inhabitants."

CHAPTER 7
THE BUILDING OF A NEW SYSTEM

A look into the future, to a new world as they see it, is one thing that the animal rights leaders must keep hidden from society. It is a future so bleak, that they would immediately be recognized as the purveyors of death the destruction that they really are.

Human logic must conclude that before a decision is made to destroy a system, some thoughts should be made to the building of a new system to replace it.

Although the animals rights ideology can give countless reasons to destroy our present system of interdependence between man and animal, and are working very effectively to dismantle that system, they give virtually no hints as to how a new system could be built to replace it. They give no answers to the problems that would be created by the "liberation" of animals.

To face these problems would require an understanding of what impacts the animal rights ideology would have on our environment. Unfortunately, a look into the future is one thing that the animal rights leaders must keep hidden from society. It is a future so bleak, that they would immediately be recognized as the purveyors of death and destruction that they really are.

Animal rights leaders recognize the fact that our present system is really made up of different herds with different shepherds managing each herd. The trapper manages one herd, the hunter another and the farmer still another. To weaken and ultimately destroy the whole system, they must eliminate the shepherds and scatter the herds.

Because the smaller herds produce less wealth and have fewer shepherds, they are recognized as the weakest part of the system. Also, because these herds are smaller, the carnage that is produced from the scattering of these herds is less apparent and easier to hide from the public.

It should have been easy to predict that the sealing industry would be their first point of attack. Its shepherds were a simple, poor and isolated culture with a naive trust in people. When the sophisticated, camera wielding, public relations experts descended on them like a plague of locusts, they had no defense. They were the real lambs being led to slaughter.

Suddenly, this small and fragile culture, made up of proud white Newfoundlanders, Inuit and Indians, was presented to the world as vicious, sadistic, bloodthirsty savages. And, they were portrayed as such, in large part, by Americans who already had the blood of an Indian culture on their hands . . . the American Indian.

In what was totally an emotional appeal to "save the seals" several unique cultures are being destroyed. The Inuit seal hunters have now become wards of the state. They are losing their will to live, and their great pride is like a candle giving off its last flicker of light, that will be lost to the next generation. Like the American Indian, they have not only been defeated, they have been humiliated and degraded. White Newfoundland fishermen, and Magdalene Islanders, have likewise suffered great economic loss, damage to fish stocks and the damage to pride that poverty brings.

The shepherds have been destroyed. What has happened to the herd? They still survive, but the first signs of their suffering and ultimate demise are starting to show. They have exhausted many of their feeding grounds, and the herd is starting to disperse. Recently they have started to appear in areas well outside their normal range in their search for new feeding and breeding grounds. More and more sickly animals are being seen, and their apparent overpopulation is beginning to take its toll of suffering and death. We can only hope they don't wither and die like their shepherds, but their chances grow less with each new day.

Unfortunately, in our fast-paced modern society, old news is no news. They have "saved the seals"; now they must take the next step in the march towards "Animal Liberation."

It has turned out that the next step taken was toward

the fur industry. Although furbearers make up a larger herd with more shepherds, the fur industry has been falsely portrayed as a vicious, bloodthirsty business. In fact, every tactic used to destroy the seal industry has been used against the wild fur industry. The animal rights forces have been honed in battle. You can see the blood in their eyes.

But gone are the innocent, trusting and naive souls that shepherded the seal herds; suddenly they face shepherds that are no longer like innocent lambs willing to be led to slaughter to feed a corrupt moral ideology. Trappers, like their ancestors the mountain men, know how to fight back and survive.

Suddenly the "animal liberators" are being asked questions they can't answer. The animal rights movement was built not on scientific principles, experience or knowledge, but rather on a faith in an ideology. But faith alone cannot provide answers.

The questions now being asked are; if trapping is eliminated what happens to the herd? What happens when animals become overpopulated and start destroying our crops? Who is going to shepherd these species and keep them from dying of starvation and disease? And no less important; what is going to happen to the shepherds?

There are no real answers. The present herd management system has evolved over thousands of years, and is the model of efficiency, with a long record of success. That success is being recognized as a balance between the herd and its habitat.

Although the animal rights groups USE individuals with degrees in animal management to push their cause, such people have little or no practical field experience, and are not recognized by the true experts in the field of wildlife management and animal husbandry as legitimate and viable authorities. This fact makes it impossible for them to formulate an alternate system. To do so would only serve to show their ignorance and prejudices. When strongly pressed to answer some of these questions asked by hunters and trappers, they prefer to raise the discussion to the higher level of emotionalism, which invariably brings the dialogue back to their arguments that any use of animals is cruel and unnecessary. This is a tactic used with considerable skill. Using this tactic, they place young men and women, who are highly trained in debate methods but little else, on an equal footing with highly experienced wildlife biologists, with little fear of being exposed for their lack of real knowledge on the subject of animals. IN FACT, BY PUTTING SUCH PEOPLE IN PUBLIC FORUM WITH WILDLIFE PROFESSIONALS, THEY ARE RECOGNIZED BY THE PUBLIC AS EXPERTS OF ANOTHER, PERHAPS EQUAL KIND.

Animal rights leaders are usually the ones to instigate these debates, resulting in an unequal forum, and resulting in an audience that is taken from ignorant urban populations at best, or is made up largely of animal rights supporters at worst. The fact that the moderators of such debates are usually sympathetic to the cause, or at least incapable of asking or demanding the answer to hard questions, puts the ultimate value of such debates solidly in the corner of the animal rights forces.

As a result of this situation, it is very hard to even speculate as to what kind of system, if any, these people would formulate to replace the present system of herd management.

So, the questions remain unanswered. In the balance of this book I will emphasize the importance these questions hold in the future of all wildlife policies, and the potential for disaster that could come from ignoring these issues.

CHAPTER 8

ANIMAL RIGHTS-- A CLASS STRUGGLE

Animal rights is really a battle that pits the movie star against the trapper - the highly educated and elitist ideologue against the farmer - the media elite against the hunter - the consumer against the producer. It is an uneven battle that pits the rich against the poor, the powerful against the weak and the famous against the unknown.

I stated in the forward of this book that the animal rights movement is a struggle between two groups of people, with two totally different philosophies concerning animals. The most troublesome aspect of the animal rights movement is that it is really a class struggle which pits the very top economic levels of society against the lower levels.

The animal rights movement is very much an elitist movement. Throughout history, it was the rich or famous who kept the idea of animal liberation alive. It did not start at the lower two thirds of society, because it is only on these lower levels that the burden of such a philosophy would be carried.

An old trapper once told me; "the easiest cause in the world to support is the one that doesn't affect you." In one simple sentence he summed up the essence of the modern animal rights movement.

It is a movement that asks for sacrifices, but the only true sacrifices required are from the lower two thirds, and more specifically, the lower third of society who have no voice in the matter, and to whom survival alone is the only cause they are concerned with.

It is these people who have the most to sacrifice, if the interaction of our herds is interrupted. A higher price on beef resulting from increased predation, or damage to crops caused from uncontrolled wildlife, will not affect people who dine on escargot, caviar and lobster. It will affect those people who even now, can only afford hamburgers and hot dogs as their source of meat.

While the movie stars ask their level of society to sacrifice the luxury of fur coats, they force trappers, hunters and fur farmers to give up their source of income and their profession. One gives up luxury while the other gives up substance.

The whole of the animal rights movement was founded and thrives financially because it draws its support from the so called socially elite of our society, which holds the wealth, prestige, fame and power. People who, I should also add, have not only made a total separation from nature, but also from the "common" man. It was this social hierarchy, made up of movie and television stars, wealthy socialites, cartoonists and well known personalities from the television news media, that has enabled the animal rights zealots to spread their propaganda throughout our society.

Although the animal rights movement has more than its share of radicals, as exemplified by the Charles Manson cult, it is this group of social elitists who provide the real power, money and influence which "fuels" the movement.

So powerful is this social dominance that those people who, in a sense straddle the social fence, are quick to sever their ties to the lower levels of society, which in many ways produced their rise in social standings. I am talking, of course, about the famous fur designers, modeling agencies, famous models, etc. who have suddenly "seen the light" of animal rights.

It is really a battle that pits the movie star against the trapper; the highly educated and elitist ideologue against the farmer; the media elite against the hunter; the consumer against the producer. It is an uneven battle that pits the rich against the poor; the powerful against the weak; and the famous against the unknown.

Nothing makes a trapper and fur farmer more angry than to have a movie or television star, who makes more money in six months than the trapper or farmer could make in three lifetimes, draw their names and professions through the mud. It is the ultimate form of social elitism.

Nothing makes a farmer, who chose his profession because he likes working with animals, more angry than to have a city born and bred ideologue, accuse him of animal abuse and neglect. It is INSULT, and the ultimate form of intellectual elitism.

Nothing makes hunters, who have spent billions of dollars to improve animal habitat, more angry than to have the city media portray them as vicious slobs. It is the ultimate form of moral elitism.

What makes the animal rights movement an elitist cause is the reality that the participants look OUTSIDE their own social circles for the problems inherent to our society. What they apparently see is a barbaric, vicious and "crude" society which manifests itself in the predatory behavior best illustrated by the practice of animal usage. In virtually all animal rights literature the basic premise is that greater reverence for animal life will lead to greater social progress and higher social ethics.

It is this obviously "superior" attitude on the part of animal rights leaders, and more importantly their financial supporters, that greatly disturbs the hunter, trapper and farmer. They recognize the fact that the long, hard (if successful) climb up the social ladder usually requires a more vicious "predatory" behavior than can be found in any other part of society. To reach the top levels of society, whether it is social, economic or the entertainment community requires a greater "hunter" (although in these circles it's referred to as "competitive") instinct than will ever burn in the hearts of most hunters, trappers and farmers.

Even those people who have inherited their social or economic position often have to recognize the fact that it took vicious and often callous behavior on the part of their predecessors to achieve that social or economic position. Although many people may suggest that it is a sense of "guilt" caused by their personal or family history that motivates these people, the fact that they prefer to ignore and deny their own social "sins" while working to effect change only on the lower levels of society proves their elitist attitudes.

Many people look at the animal rights ideology as a way by which the social elitist in our society can block out the real problems of the lower classes. By concentrating on a cause that promises to end the suffering of animals, they can safely divert their attentions, and soothe their consciences, to the plight of the poor, neglected and homeless of our society. But by so doing they often unknowingly place more burdens on those people, as is often the case in a class struggle.

Animal rights leaders are constantly comparing their movement to the civil rights movement, and the struggle for woman's equality, in an obvious effort to draw the support of all well recognized minority groups. These people must understand that "animal liberation" is a call to place even greater burdens on the human oppressed.

It's becoming increasingly apparent that the socially elite of our society have become so self-absorbed and self-important, that they now feel a need to dictate their morals to the less fortunate. Like ancient royalty, they have lost contact with the lower levels of society, and by listening to people who suggest they have the answer to the ills of the masses, their power is being used to harm society rather than help it.

CHAPTER 9
LEGISLATING THE NEW MORALITY

Never in the history of the American government has there been such a blatant manipulation of our system to serve the moral convictions of a tiny "religious" minority.

Few things are more disturbing in the animal rights movement than the apparent efforts to force their new morality through legislation. History is full of examples of small groups of people promoting, and sometimes passing, laws based on their own morals and ethics.

Queen Mary of England tried to force her religious morals on her subjects by forcing a state religion, even to the point of removing some heads. So rebellious were some of her subjects, that they fled their homeland and ultimately formed a new nation based on the principle that a man's religious beliefs were to be a personal decision.

There is no better example of a corrupt moral philosophy than "the ends justify the means," if the methods used to achieve those ends are socially harmful. Through immoral acts of human domination and butchery, Queen Mary tried to force her personal beliefs on others, and in so doing illustrated her own basic moral corruption. Even with all her power she failed, and ultimately started the decline of her nation's place in the world.

Still later, a small band of suffragettes, preaching the evils of drink, forced our nation into five years of prohibition that changed the face of America for all time. Instead of giving birth to new moral standards, it forced rebellion, and gave birth to organized crime that plagues us to this very day.

Numerous laws which promote "higher" moral standards have been written, and largely accepted as "morally right." Civil rights laws are an example. But for such laws to become a part of our moral fabric, the adoption of such laws must be a collective decision made by a majority of society.

"New" moral standards are seldom new, but rather are

a return to a moral standard that was lost somewhere along the way. Our forefathers originally understood and rejected slavery. In fact, they left Europe because they recognized themselves as slaves to royalty. But they were quick to form a new moral philosophy that justified their own use of slaves, and in a sense became no better than the masters who had enslaved them. The civil rights movement is not a crusade for a new morality, but is simply A RETURN to morality.

The animal rights issue is a new and different ideology that goes against most accepted moral standards in effect since the dawn of man. Animal rights doctrines are being built on a base of emotions, and a call for "higher" morals. On those grounds it qualifies as a form of new religion.

Although this new "religion" has been offered many times throughout history, it also has been rejected many times. It was rejected as a perverted religious ideology throughout the centuries because, until recent history, man understood animals and their place in nature. The mere fact that a large percentage of modern men have lost that understanding does not make that religion more morally acceptable, but rather allows that religion to form and grow on the very dangerous grounds of ignorance and lack of understanding.

Animal rights doctrines were formulated by people who have basically lost contact with animals and have a distorted idea of animals, the nature of animals or the role they play in nature. Likewise, most of their followers and supporters come from urban areas where their experience is totally limited to the most subservient animals of all . . . their pets.

Like the suffragettes, this small group of moral elitists is making a determined effort to force the new religion of animal rights on a society that doesn't fully understand it, and in numerous cases continues to reject it. Instead of going out and preaching the gospel of animal rights, and simply presenting their views openly, fully and honestly, they have decided to force their religion on the American people through back door politics, emotional blackmail, terrorism and subversion.

Unlike the animal rights groups, I do not make such wild claims unless I can back them up. As I proceed to do so, a very different view of their "moral superiority" will emerge from the mists in which they have cloaked themselves.

Society must look at proposed new moral standards, and new ethics, with great skepticism, especially when presented and promoted by a small group of moral elitists, who like Queen Mary, feel that the end justifies the means.

The animal rights groups are constantly comparing their movement to the civil rights movement of the 60's. They carelessly compare the black's struggle for equality, to what they view as the exploitation and repression of animals. The comparison is an insult to the noble cause of civil rights. It is, of course, a blatant and unscrupulous attempt to draw blacks, women and other minorities into the animal rights movement.

To compare women and minorities to animals in any way, is a regression back to the early days of slavery, when blacks were considered by their owners as little more than chattel. Anyone who truly knows and understand animals, knows also that any comparison of animals to humans is prejudicial to humans, and does not raise the status of animals, but rather lowers the dignity of man.

The animal rights ideology towards medical research is a good example of their prejudice against humans. Animal rights advocates have said, on numerous occasions, that a healthy animal shouldn't be sacrificed to save a sick human. Although that statement was intended to illustrate their desire for equality between humans and animals, it better illustrates their disregard for human life. The animal rights groups will defend a mother bear's right to fight and kill a human to save her cubs, but are demanding that we give up that defense, known as animal research, for our own children. In effect, the mother bear has a greater right than a human mother.

Virtually no active hunter or trapper in the world feels that what he is doing is morally wrong. There is nothing in either the Jewish or Christian teaching that even suggests that animals should be placed on an equal level with man. The average trapper and hunter has no objection to Hindu religious convictions against the killing of animals. In fact, we do not object to the fact that animal rights followers will not kill animals or eat their flesh. We are not forcing anyone to become hunters, trappers or farmers. It is entirely up to each person's own moral and religious convictions, based on his own cultural background.

If the Catholic Church were to attempt to force into law any of the proposed legislation presented by the animal rights groups, it would place society in an uproar. It would be recognized that they were trying to force their moral and religious convictions on those who don't necessarily hold those same convictions. The question is, does the animal rights religion, even though it isn't classified as such at this time, have the right to do virtually the same thing?

At this time, March 1990, there are ten bills, presented by the animal rights groups, in the Pennsylvania legislature waiting for action. In other states there is even more pressure to legislate the animal rights morality.

These people realize that by sheer numbers alone, a few of these hundreds of bills are sure to pass, and next year they will follow them with hundreds more. Never in the history of the American government has there been such blatant manipulation of our system to serve the moral convictions of a tiny "religious" minority.

An even more flagrant manipulation of our system is evident in the animal rights groups' use of terrorism and intimidation to force their "new" morals. Just recently a research laboratory at the University of California suffered damages amounting to 3.5 million dollars. It was said by the district attorney's office in California that those animal rightists, who broke into the laboratory, were the third worst terrorist group in the state. In thirty eight states, after animal rights advocates infringed on the rights of hunters, bills have been passed that make it unlawful for people to harass hunters in the field. On the federal level, Senate Bill 727 was recently passed, which makes breaking into research facilities a federal crime. Two other bills are pending in Congress to protect farmers and farm research facilities from terrorist attacks.

Can any movement be pure in its intentions, if laws must be written to protect people from the violence and harassment of that movement?

There are few people who follow the animal rights movement who don't recognize it as a thinly-veiled religious crusade.

The following letter was sent out by: The Committee to Abolish Sport Hunting, PO Box 43, White Plains, NY 10605. Written by Luke A. Dommer, President. Dated Feb. 15, 1990.

It is a clear example of the manipulation of our legal system to promote the animal rights cause. It is also an example of the constant efforts to present animals through illusion. Note the upper case words.

Fellow Anti-Hunter CRUSADERS,

I would like to take this time to bask in glory of the recent victories that we have won. It is because of you, our loyal supporters, that we have won these BATTLES.

We have closed down the sport of hunting bear and mountain lion in the state of California, and are ever so close in Colorado, Montana, Wyoming, Idaho and Washington. We have achieved this by USING THE LEGAL SYSTEM and FORCING environmental studies. How this is accomplished is that the state is mandated by law to publish its findings of the actual species herd size that is resident in the area in which they are going to hunt. This is based on a pre-determined ratio established by the COURTS. The state petitions the right to hunt that area.

What we have found is that states do not have the funding nor man-power or time required to accomplish this. So, that species remains closed for hunting. They must comply for a period of 10 years in succession. We have essentially closed THE RIGHT to hunt bear and mountain lion indefinitely in the state of California. We plan to do the same in the other afformentioned states also.

We have other exciting information to bring you. We are planning to do the same in the state of Illinois, but for whitetail deer hunting. That's right, BAMBI will be safe from all those cruel hunters. We first must concentrate our efforts on the sport of bowhunting. The bowhunters in the state are UNORGANIZED.

All of this I have told you is happening at such a rapid rate that we are building LARGE LEGAL FEES. We need your help in our fight by sending us tax deductible donations. REMEMBER BAMBI, and YOGI THE BEAR are depending on you. Our legal staff is depending on you too.

CHAPTER 10
PRESENTING THE ANIMAL RIGHTS ILLUSIONS

People are usually shocked, and their emotions stirred, by things that are foreign to their comfortable environment, by things they no longer fully understand, and no longer have to face every day.

The first step in any crusade is the education of the masses to the ideology of your movement. Once we recognize the characteristic of the Marxist-Leninist system on which the animal rights movement has been modeled, the propaganda techniques they use to educate society to their ideas become very familiar.

Like the system that it emulates, the animal rights movement has started to indoctrinate society to the idea that animals are COMMUNITY PROPERTY. To do this they have denied hunters and trappers the right to own and control our wild animals. It logically follows that the animal rights movement is a call for society to end, what they view, the unfair exploitation of these oppressed creatures by hunters, trappers and farmers, who are a minority in society.

It is obvious that the goal of animal rights is to ultimately make all our herds, (the furbearers, game animals, livestock and even pets) the collective property of society. Animal rights leaders obviously feel that this nationalization of our animals is historically inevitable, and control of our animal systems will be governed by an elite party which presumably represents the people. What better example of a Communist system ? The animal rights movement is obviously a thinly-veiled struggle for power. By manipulating society's perceptions of the present shepherd/herd systems; by offering a new moral ideology concerning animals; by convincing people of the corruption of our present systems as they see it, they place themselves in the position to seize power over our animal herds.

To accomplish this, great efforts have been made to imply that the present keepers of the herds have been derelict in their duties. That they have been so greedy in their desire to exploit animals that they have become cruel and unfeeling.

In a modern society that has lost its understanding of the age-old systems of shepherds and herds, it is apparent that the animal rights message has found very fertile ground in which to root and grow.

It is a common statement by animal rights leaders that trappers and hunters resist their call for animal liberation because they hold a vested financial interest in the continuation of their industries. They suggest that hunters have spent billions of dollars for restocking, study and habitat improvement only because it gives them more animals to kill.

In true fact, the trapper and hunter inherited their positions as shepherds of the herds. No other group in society ever asked for the responsibility of maintaining these herds, so it was left to the only people, who for centuries were the only group to value our wild animal populations, to shoulder this burden. It should be understood that even today, the animal rights groups are not asking for the awesome responsibility to maintain and nurture our wild animal herds, but rather are demanding that hunters and trappers relinquish their responsibility and control and then abandon them. It is only after this has been accomplished, that this power vacuum that would be created would have to be filled.

For centuries, society recognized and even honored hunters and trappers for their commitment as shepherds of the herd, but somehow we have lost touch with the realities of the shepherd and herd system. Although the animal rights groups constantly suggest that it is a one-sided system that only benefits a small group of individuals, it is the ultimate example of a system of give and take.

In the shepherd system the hunter and trapper must protect and nurture the herd. To do this they have spent billions of dollars, and millions of man hours building and maintaining shelter for the herds, through the purchase and maintenance of wildlife habitat. Through organizations such as Ducks Unlimited, Man the Shepherd has kept the public aware of the destruction of prime animal habitat and the fouling of the streams, rivers and marshes on which animal life depends. Long before the modern ecology movement, these shepherds saw firsthand the destruction to our planet caused by a society that did not value nature as they did. For years, their voice was like a voice from the wilderness; often unheard and unheeded, but always there.

The shepherd has also maintained the health of the herd through careful monitoring by highly trained biologists. Through the efforts of these shepherds, lost animal populations were replenished, and existing herds were maintained at a healthy level. In spite of claims to the contrary, once these good shepherds shouldered the responsibility of shepherding a species, its survival was almost assured. Not one animal in the shepherd's herd has been pushed to extinction once placed under their stewardship; an enviable record considering the great pressure mankind has exerted on many animal species through destruction of their habitat.

As a grain of corn that is planted and cultivated produces hundreds of grains in return, animals produce in excess. One pair of muskrats can produce over a hundred offspring in their lifetime, although it is only required that they produce two to replace themselves. The other ninety eight are excess that will either be harvested or left to waste. It is only from the excess that the shepherd takes a small portion as a reward for his efforts, and to sustain the over-all effort further for the good of both herd and habitat.

The animal rights groups have achieved their greatest propaganda successes by depicting hunters and trappers as cruel and unfeeling in their treatment of animals.

As a larger portion of society becomes separated from the herd, the realities that are represented by the herd become foreign to us. Although many people are repulsed by the idea of a shepherd killing and skinning his animals, it goes far beyond that. Most city people are even repulsed by the smell of manure, or even the idea of a cow being separated from its calf, while these are realities that farmers live with every day.

At the opposite extreme, when many rural people visit the city they are shocked by the homeless people huddled along the streets, and are frightened by dope addicts that call the city streets their homes; by the sight of people digging through garbage cans for their food, and the constant threat of being mugged; realities that urban populations live with every day.

To many people the reality of a human autopsy, or the dissection of a human cadaver, is repulsive, but society doesn't condemn doctors and their students for performing such procedures.

People are usually shocked, and their emotions stirred, by things that are foreign to their environment, by things they no longer fully understand, and no longer have to face every day.

Society's separation from these realities of animal life provides the animal rights groups with their very best propaganda tools. This very separation of urban and rural lifestyles results in culture shock when different people observe each other's ways.

By first describing hunting, trapping and farming as inherently cruel and vicious, animal rights groups plant the seed of doubt on the whole shepherd-herd system. When they seemingly prove those accusations with vivid descriptions, and graphic photos, they are able to manipulate normal human emotions to serve their cause.

So shocking and gross are the animal liberators' depictions of hunting and trapping that human emotions are often raised to such a high level that they become incapable of logical thought.

It would logically follow that if trapping for example, was as inherently cruel as these people describe it to be, factual depictions of the activity should be enough to destroy the fur industry overnight. In spite of this, the animal rights groups have chosen to enhance and exaggerate their descriptions of trapping to totally inaccurate and irrational levels.

Although the history of the animal rights movement is full of such exaggerated descriptions of hunting and trapping, their greatest insult to human intelligence came to light in the final days of their fight to eliminate the steel trap in New Jersey. It was no doubt their last ditch effort at emotional blackmail to force people to accept their cause, and will likely be used again at the opportune time, when they make their final push to influence people's minds.

In a large New Jersey newspaper, the animal rights groups ran an advertisement which showed a man standing in front of a snarling coyote in a trap. The caption read; This man is about to administer "the throat thrust" which is commonly used to kill animals in traps. A long sharpened stick is thrust down the coyotes throat. etc., etc.

So repulsive was the mere thought of administering death in this manner that even trappers were sickened by it. Such a description had to have come from a very sick mind, and it had to have come from the mind of an animal liberator, because nowhere in all of trapping literature is such a method of killing animals described. It's the most obvious example of the animal rights philosophy that "the end justifies the means."

So emotionally disturbing was this falsified depiction of trapping, that few people took time to logically question its authenticity. The first question would have to be; what benefit would a trapper gain by killing an animal in this manner? It would be a very slow death caused by massive bleeding. It would mean that the trapper would have to either cut and sharpen the pole before use, or he would have to carry this fairly large stick around on his trapline. There is also the question of whether an animal would stand still long enough to allow the trapper to plunge the pole deep enough to cause death. It is seldom that a wild animal would open its mouth for you long enough to drive a stake down its throat.

The common method of killing larger animals is to shoot the animal in the brain with a small caliber bullet from a revolver. It causes instant death with a minimum of bleeding. Although it does produce a small hole in the pelt, the head portion of the hide is seldom used anyway.

There's an old saying; "a picture is worth a thousand words." But today, through technical manipulation, film makers can use pictures to take us to the outermost reaches of the universe. They can make animals talk and give humans magical or super human powers. Through the use of film they can make a make believe world seem like reality.

I should state here that one of the essential ingredients that goes into the making of all film, the only exception is video film, is a gelatin that is made from hog and calf skins and animal bones. Approximately 3.5 million TONS of this material is used each year to produce camera and movie film. In reality, this makes movie and television stars, and animal rights groups who use photos in their advertising to illustrate animal abuse, as well as virtually every American, active members of the animal user groups. (2)

Just as film can be made to educate and entertain society, it can, and is, being used as a propaganda tool by animal rights groups. Because a photographic image can be easily manipulated to present a distorted image of reality it can easily be said that; "a picture is worth a thousand lies." Just as the Russians once used photos of homeless people to show their people an "example" of life in the United States, the animal rights groups use carefully staged photos and out-right lies to describe trapping, hunting and farming practices.

There are numerous examples of animal rights groups using carefully staged photos to illustrate examples of animal cruelty. An example of this "illusion" given as fact is shown at the end of this chapter.

The ultimate reason for this propaganda is to justify the call for society to provide a voice for these oppressed creatures. The "voice" is of course, animal rights groups. These groups are now demanding to have a voice in various wildlife governing boards, game commissions, etc., which would cause complete chaos.

This is inevitable because such organizations are democratic institutions, which reach their decisions through a consensus of opinion. Animal rights groups are elitist organizations which exist to gain power over man's social and spiritual evolution. They are not controlled by member votes; policies are formed by executives and staff who base their decisions on the proven marketability of their statements.

Hunters and anglers spent a record $624 million on state licenses and permits in 1986. Participation in fishing increased and hunting dipped slightly from the previous year, according to statistics released today by U.S. Fish and Wildlife Service Director, Frank Dunkle.

"Once again, hunters and anglers have made a major contribution to fish and wildlife conservation," Dunkle said. "When state license payments are added to the record $248 million these sportsmen paid in federal excise taxes for their equipment last year, the total is an impressive $872 million, all earmarked for fish and wildlife programs.

U.S. Department of Interior fish and Wildlife Service, 1986.

THE ILLUSION

This photo, used by a number of animal rights groups has been, without doubt, one of the most widely seen and most effective fund raising tool in the history of the animal rights movement. It is; "A photo worth millions of dollars." Wildlife experts consider it to be a total ILLUSION. The image has been used as propaganda that preys on the ignorance of its viewers, and I consider it an insult to human intelligence. It appears to be a poorly staged photo that uses an apparently road killed raccoon. The discrepancies are as follows:

1. Although the raccoon foot is badly mangled...there is no BLOOD on the foot, trap, or fur. How could an animal be this badly injured and not bleed?
2. The size of the trap seems illogical. The length of the trap is equal to the length of the raccoon. In most eastern states this size trap is illegal to use by state law. Most raccoon are taken in much smaller devices.
3. Although the raccoon would appear to have been in the trap for some time, the trap is not marked. When animals are held for a prolonged time in a trap they scrape, scratch and chew off the dark coloration on the trap producing a "shine."
4. The surface on which the raccoon was laid is obviously asphalt. Nowhere in this photo can be found a twig, leaf or ground debris that would normally be dug up in its struggle. Animals are not trapped on asphalt.
5. Although animal rights groups suggest that animals "chew" the foot to escape, there is no indication of this in the photo.

THE REALITY

This is a far more typical illustration of a trapped raccoon. Note the obvious differences in the size of the trap, ground conditions, etc. Note also, the lack of injury on this animal. Modern, appropriately sized traps only restrain the animal. They are seldom visibly injured.

CHAPTER 11
PESTS AND PREDATORS

This indoctrination of our youth to the animal rights ideology can only be compared to the brainwashing of China's youth after the Communist Revolution.

The animal rights movement survives and flourishes because we have increasingly become an urbanized society. Most city dwellers get their whole education concerning animals from their television sets or from books written and produced by city people, who often know no more about animals than their viewers and readers; a perfect example of the blind leading the blind. To say that this has given millions of Americans a distorted picture of wildlife would be putting it mildly indeed.

Such depictions of animal life are often no more realistic, or factually depicted, than the T.V. program "Cosby" depicts life in Harlem. Even "so called" wildlife programs, show only the good side of nature. Heaven forbid that they show the starving, diseased animals of the real world. Unfortunately, none of these shows are required to state that what you see is a real life event. The closest they come is to declare that it was a depiction of what they describe as real animal behavior.

Just as important, the trapper and hunter have suddenly replaced the "Big Bad Wolf" as the essence of evil in modern fairy tales. Each has replaced the "savage redskin" as the essence of crude blood lust. More and more, trappers and hunters are depicted as vicious monsters in T.V. programs, cartoons, children's books and even in adult novels. "Seabert the Seal" is perhaps the most blatant example of this as a children's program. This indoctrination of our youth to the animal rights ideology can only be compared to the brainwashing of China's youth after the Communist Revolution. It's a shameless effort to pervert the natural love of animals, which all children share, into an often vicious hate for the people who harvest and care for them. The animal rights fanatics are so twisted in their morals, that they have started playing with our children's minds. Animal rights leaders understood from the very beginning that their real strength lay in the cities. This is a strength based on the urban populations' ignorance and indifference towards animals. They recognized the city dweller as the perfect victim to exploit with their brainwashing techniques, and have spent millions of dollars in their efforts to "educate" people to their doctrines.

From the very beginning of the modern American movement, animal rights leaders have used state and federal representatives from urban districts to do their bidding. Although a huge majority of city dwellers have no interest in the animal rights movement, a small group of active and very vocal participants in the movement have convinced these politicians to introduce endless legislation to outlaw hunting or trapping, or at least to hamper their activities.

The perceived power of the animal rights groups becomes apparent when it is realized that such legislation does not appear to affect the constituents of the urban politician in any way. In fact, these representatives feel free to introduce such legislation simply because they do not have to answer to trappers, hunters and livestock farmers, who are not a part of their constituency. Few people would disagree that this is an abuse of their power that our founding fathers never intended.

What urban dwellers do not realize is that eventually the animal rights movement will affect them, far more than being harassed for wearing a fur coat on the streets.

Most city dwellers do not realize that in every port city, and most inland cities, they host a greater population of wild animals per square mile than virtually any rural area in the U.S. I'm talking, of course, about rats and mice. In many cities, the population of these rodents has reached epidemic proportions.

At present, a degree of control is being exerted on these rodents through the use of poison, glue strips and various traps. What people don't realize is that none of these control measures are acceptable to the animal rights groups.

After all, is it any more acceptable for the city dweller to take the life of an animal than it is for a hunter and trapper?

Although most people will scoff at the idea of protection of rats and mice, it must be understood that much of the same danger produced by an overpopulation of rodents in our cities, is also present in rural areas from overpopulations of wildlife.

Just as city people would not want rats and mice contaminating and destroying their food supplies, farmers do not want coon, deer, woodchuck, beaver, etc. destroying their crops (ultimately the food for city dwellers).

Just as city residents fear the spread of disease from rats, rural people fear the spread of disease from wildlife to their family, pets and livestock.

Just as city people need exterminators to control pests, farmers need trappers and hunters to control wildlife.

It's been suggested that the present growth of the rat population in our cities is due to the availability of trash and garbage. As long as rats have an abundant supply of food available, their population will flourish. Likewise, as long as farmers have crops in their fields many of the animals that destroy those crops will flourish. As long as cattle and sheep are put out to pasture coyotes will continue to kill and eat them.

What many city people don't realize is that the animal rights people have come up with what they feel is the answer to the problem of rats in our city, and the deer in our crops . . . birth control! When this idea was presented to a sheep farmer in the West who was having problems with coyotes killing his sheep, he answered; "They're not breeding my sheep, they're eating them."

He immediately understood what the animal rights supporters don't. If he has six coyotes in his sheep pasture, and you have six big rats in your home, feeding them birth control pills won't change their nuisance value; the coyotes will continue to kill sheep, and the rats will still be digging in your partitions.

Sure, the complete protection of rats and mice is a

ridiculous idea ... just as ridiculous as the complete "protection" of wildlife.

CHAPTER 12

ANIMAL RESEARCH

Animal rights groups depend on the collective ignorance of the American people, not their collective knowledge. It is a movement that thrives in the darkness of ignorance. Once the light of knowledge and understanding shines on the animal rights movement it will wither and die.

Possibly the most radical and terroristic groups in the animal rights movement are those which protest the use of animals for medical research. The most notorious of these groups is the Animal Liberation Front (ALF) which has publicly threatened to use terrorism to achieve their objectives. It is obvious that they are already making good on that threat. Numerous medical laboratories have been burned and destroyed, and research animals set free, or carried away. So brazen are these groups that they videotape their illegal activities, then send copies to the television networks which use them to illustrate, what they view, as the selfless devotion of these self-righteous radicals.

Few people would suggest that most proponents of animal rights are not experts on animals, and seldom do they promote themselves as such. In their eyes, their moral and intellectual superiority are all the reasons they need to justify their terroristic activities.

I am not a doctor or scientist, so I am not qualified to testify on the subject of medical research. To do so woul[d] put me in the same category as the animal rights leaders.

In spite of my ignorance on the subject, I do have a f[air] share of common sense and logic, and after all, that i[s] that is needed to expose the perverted ideology of the [ani]mal rights movement. In fact, that is what this book [is] about. It is an effort to push aside the emotional ve[il that] blinds people to the corrupt ideology presented by [animal] rights leaders. The animal rights groups depen[d on the] collective ignorance of the American people, not [their col]lective knowledge. It is a movement that thri[ves in the] darkness of ignorance. Once the light of kno[wledge]

understanding shines on the animal rights movement, it will wither and die.

Nothing in the animal rights movement seems more illogical to me than their call to end medical research on animals. To place the welfare of animals over the welfare of humans can only be described as a perverted religious doctrine, written somewhere in Hell.

Not since the days of Hitler's persecution of the Jews has a small group of people been allowed to place such a low value on human life; a value that is not even equal to the value of a laboratory rat. Think for just a moment; that is the value they have placed on YOU.

The animal rights leaders have been very successful at placing an emotional veil over our eyes. So deep are our emotions stirred by the sight of a monkey receiving a violent blow to the head; or an animal with wires and tubes protruding from its skull; or animals locked in small cages, that we forget that there are thousands of little children suffering from cancer, AIDS, burns, etc. in our hospitals, often kept in cage-like beds. We fail to think about tens of thousands of diabetics who must inject themselves with insulin each morning; or the kidney patients who must undergo kidney dialysis each week; or the cancer patients who must suffer the effects of chemotherapy. That is where real suffering can be found, and if medical experts say that suffering can be lessened through animal research than the American people have a moral obligation to support them.

I worked in a hospital for a short time, and the human suffering I saw there lives with me to this very day. I was not in the position to ease that suffering, so it affected me differently than the doctors and nurses who actively worked to ease their patients' pain and discomfort. Except in the very old patients who had resigned themselves to their fate, most terminally ill patients showed a desperate desire to live. So strong is man's will to live that most people would do almost anything to survive, even a few days. It is these people who should decide if animal research should continue. Only they can understand the

74

agony of the soul, and helplessness of the spirit, that comes from knowing they will die before their time. We have no right to make this decision for them, or the thousands of people who will find themselves in the same situation in the future. Who can tell them that we couldn't use every method possible to save their lives? At that time the proponents of animal rights won't be found, and the job will be left to the doctors whose hands were tied.

By virtue of the very existence of the animal rights ideology, we have become a very sick society, but I refuse to believe that our opinions of ourselves, and our fellow man, have sunk so low that we will continue to allow this sick religious ideology to invade our lives.

The danger is that most people do not realize that it is invading our lives more and more with each passing day, and ultimately will affect the lives of every person reading this book.

Society must realize that the animal rights ideology is INVADING our lives. Terrorists who burn and destroy medical laboratories did not ask your permission; research projects were not canceled because you requested it; restrictive legislation was not written with your hand; the attempted murder of medical technicians is not a mark on your soul; OR IS IT?

The sickness and moral corruption that is represented by the animal rights ideology cannot invade the body of our society, unless we allow it. Cancer starts with one tiny sick cell. Unless it is killed very early in its existence, it will continue to grow despite every effort to kill it. If this cancer called animal rights is allowed to continue its growth in our society it will produce a sickness that will weaken the moral and spiritual body of man. It will produce a sickness for which there is no cure.

CHAPTER 13

HISTORICAL CHANGES IN THE TRADITIONAL ROLE OF HUMANE SOCIETIES

While hunters and trappers are accused of needlessly "killing" animals, pet owners, vets and animal shelter workers, only "put them to sleep." Although this is an obvious form of denial to soothe our feelings, it has fostered a form of discrimination and hypocrisy within the humane groups.

Although the animal rights movement comes very close to expressing the ultimate example of moral and intellectual elitism, involvement in the cause by a few members and employees of humane societies is the ultimate example of hypocrisy.

Until the turn of the century, there is little in the historical record that would indicate that our forefathers placed any importance on pets, at least as viewed in that capacity by modern society.

In the vast majority of cases, dogs were bred for hunting, and the protection and herding of livestock. There are only a tiny number of dog and cat breeds that were developed to serve as pets, and in each case they were bred as such by the socially elite and very wealthy members of society.

Although the common house cat had long been a favorite pet of members of the higher levels of ancient societies, until the turn of the century they served a more practical function at lower income levels of society in their capacity to control rodents. To serve that role efficiently, it is doubtful that more than minimum attention was given to their needs. In fact, it would have been counterproductive to feed them too much, and their presence in the home would only be required if rodents became a problem.

I would not want to minimize the importance of rodent control before the invention and utilization of traps and poison. Food storage facilities were very crude, and because the whole winter's food supplies for both themselves and the livestock were kept in storage, damage or loss caused by rodents had to be minimized.

A hard and demanding life was typical at the lower economic levels of society in Europe and the U.S. until the turn of the century. It was a life that required long, hard hours of heavy physical work just to survive. It was only because dogs and cats served the needs of man that they retained a niche in man's environment. But to survive, every person and animal had to carry its share of the load.

In an effort to increase their value to man, dogs were carefully bred to fulfill specific needs. The Labradors and spaniels were bred to retrieve game; beagles, plotts, blueticks, etc., were bred to hunt game; the collies were bred to herd livestock at a time when fences were nonexistent or too expensive; the shepherds were bred to provide protection for livestock; etc. This wide diversity of needs ultimately produced many different breeds of dogs.

In comparison, there were very few breeds of house cats developed. Undoubtedly, the very first domestic house cat was just as efficient at controlling rodents as any modern variety. There was little need or benefit in what would, no doubt, be a fruitless effort to improve their value through breeding.

With the advent of traps and the introduction of poison as a means of controlling rodents, and better long-term storage of food, house cats became less important to man. Also, with the introduction of fencing, dogs became less useful. Fortunately, because of a higher living standard, cats and dogs found a new niche in society; they became our well-fed and pampered pets. In light of the fact that the major humane societies were founded before the turn of the century, it's apparent that their original and primary role was to eliminate abuse to livestock, which may have included dogs. With the relatively recent social trend towards greater use of animals for pets, the "S.P.C.A.," while it retains and exercises its power to intervene in cases of animal abuse, has become largely a type of society for the management of pet populations.

Although exact figures are hard to come by, it is estimated that close to 20 million unwanted dogs, cats, puppies and kittens are killed by animal shelters each year. No doubt many more are destroyed by their owners through drowning, clubbing and abandonment.

A common statement by pet owners, veterinarians and more importantly animal shelter workers, is that they put animals to "sleep." As one old farmer recently asked; "If all they're doing is putting them to sleep, when are they going to wake them up?" Our culture works hard at avoiding guilt for causing death.

While trappers and hunters are accused of needlessly "killing" animals, pet owners, vets and shelter workers, only "put them to sleep." Although this is an obvious form of denial to soothe our feeling, it has fostered a form of discrimination and hypocrisy within each humane organization.

In many local humane society chapters, we are seeing more and more evidence that they are adopting the ideology of the animal rights movement. The anti-fur movement seems to be of special interest to them. It is not uncommon to see, in their offices, a poster-size advertisement of a woman in a fur coat with blood seeping from the bottom; solid condemnation of the fur industry in general, and fur ranching in particular.

Considering the objections they voice against the practice of fur farming, namely animals in small pens, killing by electrocution and most important their objections to raising and killing animals for the sake of vanity, you have to wonder how humane societies could be so hypocritical in their views to not recognize the fact that they, in the eyes of animal rights, are making their living in fundamentally the same way as the mink rancher.

The "S.P.C.A." is first of all, just as guilty of placing animals in small pens as mink ranchers. These pens are proportionately as small for dogs and cats, as mink cages are for mink. Secondly, while the "S.P.C.A." "puts animals to sleep" mink ranchers "kill" animals with gas and injection. The fact is, humane societies "kill" un-wanted pets by methods that are no more or less brutal and painful than those methods used by mink or fox ranchers, or for that matter, trappers. These are not matters for conjecture, they undeniable truths.

The most potent argument used against fur ranching is the fact that animals are raised to satisfy human vanity. The dictionary describes vanity as: A lack of real value; worthlessness. or; a useless, idle or worthless thing. By this description a fur coat by virtue of its use as clothing, is not a vain object. Although the person who is wearing it may still be considered vain in human wants and desires, elimination of fur coats is not likely to change that person's personality.

In that light, pet ownership is no more or less vain than is owning a fur coat. Just as important, pets are not free agents. Unless they are abandoned, pets are considered by people as property. People own them.

Both of these points go directly against the animal rights ideology. Although many humane societies are crawling into bed with the animal rights groups, they are fundamentally at odds with each other. Although the animal rights groups are presently willing to use local affiliates to serve their own ends, ultimately they may become fierce enemies.

In the animal rights ideology the first thing that must go is the modern concept of man's ownership of animals. In the teachings of animal rights literature, countless examples are used to illustrate their comparison of negro slavery with man's domination of animals. The concept of "pet ownership" cannot sit well with people who consider themselves "animal liberators."

The next thing that must go is the indiscriminate ownership of pets. Although the vast majority of pet owners take very good care of their pets, even to the point of pampering them, there has always been a small number of pet owners who neglect and abuse their animals. It is logical that the first step, to the ultimate end of pet ownership, will be the elimination of indiscriminate pet ownership by people, who by virtue of their social status, financial instability, living environment and possibly even educational level, become targeted candidates as accused animal abusers. This discrimination towards pet ownership is already apparent. Recently, a local chapter of the S.P.C.A. in the state of Massachusetts refused the adoption of a dog by a known hunter, on the grounds that he would use that animal for hunting purposes.

At the moment, it is up to S.P.C.A. officials to determine who they feel are unfit to adopt animals from their shelters, but as the animal rights ideology invades these organizations, stricter and more pervasive restrictions are constantly being implemented. The initial results will naturally discriminate against the economically poorer half of human society, who by virtue of their lower living standards, fit the basic criteria as unfit for pet ownership.

In their self-described position as animal liberators, leaders of the animal rights movement, complain vigorously against the raising of ranch mink and fox in cages. Because mink and fox establish large territories in which they travel, their confinement to pens, no matter how large, goes against their natural instincts. As a result, animal rights advocates label this as a form of cruelty. It is not hard, using that kind of logic, to make the same case against cats and dogs which live in homes, apartments and kennels, which by virtue of the confinement, are not being allowed to follow their natural instincts. After all, dogs and cats would naturally establish territories at least as large as mink and fox, if allowed to roam free. (Ingrid Newkirk has cited apartment life for dogs as cruel, and has stated that they should all be freed of this slavery.)

The ultimate conflict that will have to be faced by animal rights advocates and the S.P.C.A. is the huge number of unwanted pets that must be destroyed each year. In the eyes of animal rights advocates, 20 million animal deaths each year has to be viewed as a virtual bloodbath.

Although most animal rights groups encourage the spaying and neutering of pets, by virtue of their flimsy efforts to encourage or finance such efforts, it is obvious that they recognize three fundamental flaws in this practice.

The main drawback to the practice of spaying and neutering animals is that it goes directly against the basic doctrines of animal rights. First, it causes a degree of pain and suffering in the animals. Secondly, it's a form of mutilation of innocent animals. And finally, it cannot be described as a natural process. Instead, it was a practice that was instigated not to serve animals, but to ease the responsibilities of man.

Common logic also dictates that if a species is to survive, reproduction must occur. This presents the problem of who will decide which animals must be spayed or neutered, if the practice is allowed to continue. Can a person be forced to neuter a pet dog on the grounds that it's a mixed breed? Will hunters be forced to neuter dogs because their pups may be used for the "cruel" sport of hunting? Again, the economically disadvantaged portions of society would be the first to be impacted by such a requirement. It is these levels of society that owns predominantly mixed breed dogs, and would undoubtedly be the one group to neglect the responsibility of spaying and neutering their pets because of lack of financial resources to do so.

This brings us to one inescapable conclusion. The only logical and workable plan which would stop the bloodbath represented by killing 20 million unwanted pets, is the rigid restrictions, or better still total elimination of private pet ownership.

Now, I do not personally advocate restrictions on private pet ownership. I am not willing to give up my pets to satisfy someone else's moral philosophy. I am sure that a huge majority of people agree with me. The problem lies in the hypocrisy of people who question, and condemn, the need for wildlife management, while condoning what is virtually the same practice now being conducted by humane societies. Without this management of pet populations, implemented through the mass killing of pets, huge overpopulation of dogs and cats would result. In a short time, nature would take over the job of management through starvation, exposure, disease, etc. While people understand and condone the practice when implemented on pets, a growing number of people, condemn the practice when implemented on wildlife through hunting and trapping. I personally cannot think of a better example of self serving hypocrisy.

I come into personal contact with thousands of trappers, hunters and farmers each year. I have yet to meet a single individual among these ranks who does not recognize and value the primary goals of the local S.P.C.A. We support these very worthwhile organizations, not because they provides us with a convenient way to ignore the pain, suffering and death, that are often the realities of the shepherd/herd system, but rather the service it provides for animals. In reality, most members of society recognize the value of the S.P.C.A. in human terms, in the fact that it soothes and protects human emotions and feelings from the realities of nature.

Will people, who feel that wildlife management is unnecessary and cruel, also condemn the S.P.C.A. on the same grounds? Each society for the prevention of cruelty to animals serves as a secondary shepherd of a herd just like hunters and trappers. As such, each should be supporting these groups instead of condemning them.

*According to a published report in the Union-News, Springfield, Mass., Dennis Tonguay was refused an English springer spaniel by MSPCA after he said the dog would be used for hunting. Mr. Tonguay said he figured that even if the dog was not a great hunting dog, he and the dog could provide companionship for each other while hunting in the woods.

Said Mary Beth Marquardt, manager of the Springfield SPCA shelter, "We don't adopt out for hunting because the MSPCA is against sport hunting."

According to published reports, the MSPCA puts more than 5,000 abandoned dogs to sleep each year.

CHAPTER 14
VEGETARIANISM--THE FINAL SOLUTION ?

If man can understand that prey species exist totally as a source of protien for other animals, it should not be morally offensive for man, who is by nature a predator ... to join in the feast.

It is not unreasonable to assume that the ultimate goal of the animal rights movement is a vegetarian society. Although the true motives for promoting a vegetarian community are the manipulation of human cultural and even physical evolution, modern society is not ready to understand, much less accept, such a radical concept. As a result, the most logical first step in the promotion of vegetarianism is to place animals in a position of reverence which can only be accomplished by giving them rights. After all, what greater insult could a man impose on an animal's rights than to eat its flesh?

In spite of the absurdity and flawed reasoning behind this goal, as I will soon explain, a growing number of people in Europe and the United States, are professing a commitment to living their lives as vegetarians.

Practicing vegetarians give a number of reasons for this very fundamental change in their lifestyle. In most cases, practitioners of vegetarianism site religion, morals, compassion, and recently even common logic, as grounds for their "new enlightenment."

I should first point out, the idea of living a meat-free existence, is not a new one. Many famous and influential people, through recent, and relatively ancient history, have freely and openly espoused their personal commitments to vegetarianism. Proponents of animal rights frequently use highly respected historical names as examples of committed vegetarians. They are generous in their open and implied use of the words "enlightened," "progressive," "liberated" and "compassionate" in their description of these famous people.

I am a little too humble to question the compassion of Susan B. Anthony, or the religious commitment of Gandhi, both vegetarians, but I must question the free use of their names as examples of progressive or enlightened thinking, in terms of vegetarianism. To do so would to imply that their deep concern for the spiritual and physical condition of man was somehow tied to the fact that they chose to lead their lives as vegetarians.

So self righteous are the high priests of animal rights, that in their rush to glorify their cause through the exhibition of their patron saints, they fail to recognize the most famous vegetarian of all . . . Adolph Hitler.

When you look at the social position of the more outspoken proponents of vegetarianism, a different view of the phenomenon comes into focus. Not one single case can be cited where an individual has achieved fame or prominence based, even in small part, as a result of his or her commitment to vegetarianism. In many instances, a commitment to vegetarianism is made only after such people reach a high, and more importantly a visible, social position.

In our modern society, movie and television stars, artists, philosophers and musicians are often very vocal in their commitment to a meat-free society. If a poll were taken to determine how many people in the entertainment community were avowed vegetarians, the percentages would surprise you. At the highest level of these industries, people who at least show a sympathy for such a cause would be viewed by many as a social phenomenon at that level of society.

At the opposite end of the spectrum, a poll taken in most rural areas, or in the very poor sections of our cities would find the percentage of people who have even considered the concept of vegetarianism to be virtually nonexistent. At the lower end of society, vegetarianism is still viewed as a very radical, unacceptable and foolish idea. In fact, most of these people would voice their desire to eat more meat, if they could afford it.

It is not hard to draw the conclusion that vegetarianism specifically, and animal rights generally, are ideas that originated at or near the highest social level of our populace. The socially elite of our society that is often given credit for changes in our social conduct and interests, but seldom in our social consciousness.

The betterment of society is a very noble cause; it is also a tremendous responsibility that should not, and cannot, be taken lightly. To push a cause, any cause, based on a fundamentally flawed and self-serving philosophy can be dangerous to the health of a society, and just as importantly can destroy the credibility of its proponents, who have a genuine concern for the human race and our environment. Such people may have the power to make a difference in world problems which we all face, problems that are equally shared at both ends of the social ladder.

The problem with people at the highest level of society taking fundamental, and often very visible stands on issues that concern society is their separation from society. How many people in the entertainment industry for example, are hunters, trappers, farmers or ranchers. How many of these people can count as a friend or acquaintance a farmer from Wisconsin, a rancher from Wyoming or a trapper from Canada? For such people to push a social cause that has a minimum effect on themselves or their colleagues, but has a negative effect on lower levels of society, smacks of social elitism.

The anti-fur movement is a good example. While people at the higher levels of society ask for sacrifices of a luxury ... furs, they demand greater and more devastating sacrifices at lower levels of society, from people whose very livelihood depends on the manufacture and sale of furs.

To ignore farmers, trappers and hunters on the common argument that they are motivated by their vested interest in continuation of their traditional lifestyles, also smacks of moral elitism. If proponents of vegetarianism stand on solid moral and intellectual ground, and can provide a sense of logic to those ends, the first people they should try to convert are the farmers and ranchers. Instead, they label them morally and intellectually corrupt, in effect negating their knowledge, experience and contributions to mankind.

When the words compassion, morals and ethics are

used in recruitment of people to a cause, it is frightening in its implications. Too often when a cause is built on moral grounds, or is described as the compassionate thing to do, it becomes an emotional issue that throws reason, common logic and experience to the winds.

Worse still is a cause that builds as its foundation a twisted sense of logic; twisted and perverted because it does not use knowledge or experience as a basis for that logic.

If we put aside the moral reasons for vegetarianism by simply saying that until it becomes a law, which still would not make it IMMORAL, the choice to eat meat or not to eat meat, is a PERSONAL decision.

To discontinue the eating of meat on moral ground, simply on the urging of another person, would require a great faith in the moral superiority of that person. If such an act of faith is too hard to achieve, and with most people it is, than we are left with few alternatives on which to base our decision.

The first, and quite possibly the most important, is man's understanding or lack of understanding, of animals. In our modern urban and suburban society, the whole extent of personal human involvement with animals is limited to experience with pets. In the majority of cases this means dogs, cats, and in more affluent households, riding horses.

The dog has even been given the honor of being labeled "man's best friend." Before the animal rights movement, we often read of very wealthy people leaving their fortune to their pet dog or cat; and, what young girl hasn't asked her parents for a pony or horse?

There is little doubt that this close relationship with pets has done much to nurture people's love for animals, as well it should. The problem comes when you try to view all animals in the same light that you view your own pets. To do so would be like trying to love all women as you would your own mother, an act which would make your mother's love less special, and would require no special responsibility and commitment on the part of your mother to earn that love.

There are some very fundamental differences between your dog or cat, and a cow, sheep or chicken. The most basic difference is that your dog and cat were born predators who survive by living off the flesh of other animals.

Regardless of the amount of love and respect a dog shows its master, under the right circumstances, even the most gentle dog will kill. The larger breeds are capable of killing game up to the size of deer. Smaller breeds are capable of killing rabbits, chickens, ducks, etc.

On the other hand, cattle, sheep and chickens are prey species. Their principle reason for existence is to provide feed for the predators. If turned loose in the wilds a sheep would soon be killed and eaten by predators. In fact, tens of thousands of sheep ARE killed by coyotes and dogs each year.

If man can understand that prey animals exist totally as a source of protein for other animals, it should not become morally offensive for man, who is by nature a predator, to join in the feast.

It should also be understood, that the physiology of man shows every indication that he IS a predator. The mere fact that we can digest meat; the fact that we have teeth capable of tearing and chewing flesh; the fact that we have eyes in the front of our heads, as do most predators, instead of at the sides like most prey species; the fact that unlike cattle, sheep, rabbits, etc., we actually like the taste of meat provides ample proof that we are instinctive meat eaters.

In spite of the desire by some to ignore or deny these facts, it doesn't change them. Of all the statements I have made in this book, the suggestion that we are born predators will likely offend vegetarians more than any other. There can be no more logical reason to become a vegetarian than as a form of denial that we are predators. It is the one issue that most vegetarians carefully avoid, although there are a few exceptions.

"We possess a predatory instinct, which is part of our primitive nature. However, those who have cultivated their spiritual nature are disturbed by the notion that killing for food is justifiable not withstanding our predatory instinct." (3)

Thoreau.

Virtually every argument that man makes to promote vegetarianism is a form of denial. They say that we don't need meat; that meat makes you aggressive; that eating meat shows a lack of compassion; that it shows an unnatural dominance over other animals, traits common to all known predatory animals.

The opposition to hunting and trapping are also attempts to deny the fact that man is a predator by nature. Hunting and trapping are the ultimate examples of predatory behavior. Again, proponents of animal rights, regularly call trappers and hunters bloodthirsty, barbaric, vicious, callous, unfeeling and sadistic. An almost perfect description of a predator, if viewed in a negative light. In spite of the possible benefits of calling them predators, I have yet to hear trappers and hunters described by that term by the animal rights people, which further indicates an obvious form of denial. To call any man a predator, would be a form of admission that man is governed by a predatory instinct common to ALL humans.

It logically follows that people who suffer from such denial, would tend to label those of us who openly exhibit the "hunter" instincts as a model of UNUSUAL human behavior instead of an example of normal behavior.

That is the first, and only logical reason for becoming a vegetarian, but relatively few people are suffering from this form of denial. To draw converts to your cause, you must find other reasons for them to join in. You must build a broader base of appeal. As a result of denial of their real motives, attempts to find more convenient motives are pretty feeble.

Like any other cult movement, true believers are seldom satisfied with their own feeling of enlightenment. By virtue of their small numbers, they usually feel a need to produce new converts to their beliefs. With each new convert their own beliefs and faith come one step closer to becoming accepted. Although most vegetarians view themselves as progressive, they know that they run the risk of being viewed differently by others, who don't share their beliefs. Because most of these people are very socially conscious, the initial attention they receive for being courageous enough to make a moral stand, quickly wears thin. Unless they can convert others to their beliefs they run the risk of becoming labeled radical or kooks. Because these people are usually social elitists, what the general public believes doesn't concern them. What does concern them is how they are viewed by others of their social standing.

Unfortunately, in the higher social hierarchy, and in the creative community, it is considered chic to be part of a cause, to be viewed as a crusader.

Many people reach this level of society through natural talents for which they cannot take credit. Others can see no tangible, long lasting benefits in their contributions to society. To find a cause that implies that you are filled with love and compassion soothes the conscience of those who live a life of luxury and opulence.

To such people the animal rights movement, and ultimately their personal commitment to vegetarianism which the movement forces, provides them with two things they feel are lacking in their lives. Through their avowed love of animals they are first able to demonstrate a capacity for love and compassion, and through vegetarianism they are able to soothe their conscience through sacrifice.

Because the animal rights movement provides the benefits such people are seeking, it has become the "in" thing to do, and in high social circles, as could be predicted, it has drawn many converts. But, as in all things, for every plus there is a minus.

The biggest problem faced by the animal rights movement is its inability to draw sizable numbers of converts from lower levels of society who are not driven by a sense of inadequacy, guilt, lack of love or compassion or a need to deny their basic nature as predator. For these people you need more tangible arguments.

The first of these arguments hinges on the claimed other benefits of vegetarianism. Their basic argument suggests that the production of beef is a huge waste of grains that could more logically be used to feed a growing world population. They also claim that the feeding of grain crops to cattle increases the cost of grain and reduces its availability to poor people of this world. It's even been suggested that if we stopped the raising of beef, we would no longer have to see the horrors of whole nations of starving people on our television sets.

This is, of course, a great way to tug on your heart strings, and force a sense of guilt for our abundant lifestyles. Fortunately, it simply isn't true.

Over the length and width of this earth, and in virtually every nation, there are hundreds of millions of acres of grass lands suitable only for the grazing of animals, or the production of hay to feed those animals. Due to the topography of the land, poor soil, lack of rainfall and severe weather conditions, they are virtually worthless for the production of grain or vegetables. To remove the livestock from these lands would mean the total loss of this land for the production of food.

In most poorer countries, cattle are fed little or no grain at all. In richer countries like the U.S. cattle are fed grain, but only for a relatively short time before slaughter to increase the fat content of the meat. With the present concern for cholesterol in our diets, the amount of grains fed these animals will no doubt decrease even more, in our efforts to produce leaner meats.

A more recent argument put forth by vegetarians is that beef cattle (although this would also have to apply to ALL animals) waste both water and vegetable protein and the latter is no less nutritious for man than flesh. Such statements are an insult to human intelligence. First of all, while man can only eat kernels of corn, cattle eat the cobs, husks, stalks, leaves and even the tassel. They are able to derive nutrients, minerals, vitamins, calcium, iron, etc. from those parts of the plant that are useless to man. And not only do they utilize this roughage, what they don't absorb they recycle back to the soil in the form of a high quality and faster acting fertilizer. The water used to water plants which feed the animals, or is used by the animal itself, is not "wasted" but is returned to the environment through nature's hydrologic cycle.

It should be stated here that man the predator is a MEAT eater. Unfortunately, because we have become a wealthy society we have strayed from our predatory instincts and have become FAT eaters. In reality, in warmer climates, there is very limited need for fats in our diet. In nature, the only predators which require a great deal of fat in their diets are those predators which are exposed to a very cold climate. Although man could tolerate high levels of fat in his diet if constantly exposed to the rigors of a cold outdoor climate, by the creation of an artificial climate (homes and offices) he has reduced his need for animal fats which are utilized very slowly by the body. This is especially true in a sedentary lifestyle.

The most logical answer to this is not to abandon our predatory instincts, but rather to return to them by trimming off the excess fat and eating leaner MEAT. And more importantly, get more exercise which is more natural to our predatory biological profile. In fact, numerous medical research programs have proven that the most logical cure for most of man's medical problems, including high blood cholesterol, is vigorous exercise.

Vegetarianism promotes (in their words) passivism, subservience and non-aggression as the ultimate goals for a vegetarian society, which again goes against our predatory physiology.

It should also be understood, in our new concern for our ecology, that the raising of livestock is the safest and most ecologically sound method of producing foods. By themselves, animals add relatively few pollutants to our atmosphere, very low level and non life-threatening pollutants to our water, and through their dung, actually recycle plant life back to the soil.

On the other hand, the raising of grain requires the

heavy use of pesticides, herbicides and chemical fertilizers. As the use of these chemicals become restricted, as they no doubt will, the need for meat products will increase.

On the basis of their inability to convince society to the material benefits of vegetarianism, which is non-existent, and their failure to convert the lower economic levels of society to their religious doctrines, they have started to systematically force society into vegetarianism. The first step to that end is the attack, and ultimately the destruction of our present shepherd/herd systems. Like ancient European royalty they are attempting to force a state religion.

CHAPTER 15
THE SEARCH FOR A NEW GOD

It has become increasingly apparent to me that the animal rights movement is based on a religious philosophy that is still in its formative stages, which results in a certain amount of confusion even within the movement itself.

As I started writing this book, I became more and more aware that the animal rights movement has all the characteristics of a religious crusade. This is something which trappers, especially, have suspected for some time.

I hesitate to enter into the subject of religion, but because an increasing amount of animal rights literature condemns the Judeo-Christian ethic as one of the basic causes for animal cruelty, the subject is appropriately addressed.

Animal rights leaders have been careful to cover their true motives and beliefs. In fact, a virtual army of wildlife experts, biologists, etc., have tried for years to understand the "religion" of animal rights, and have been unable to develop any clear answers.

It was while writing the earlier chapters in this book, which started simply as an examination of the animal rights movement, that the real clues to the nature of this movement began to become apparent. As I progressed through that evaluation, the veil of secrecy in which animal rights leaders have shrouded themselves began to fall away.

I am by no stretch of the imagination a religious scholar. In fact, it was only because I approached the religious issue from a position of ignorance, that I was able to recognize the true gods of animal rights. It has become increasingly apparent to me that the animal rights movement is based on a religious philosophy that is still in its formative stages, and has resulted in a certain amount of confusion even within the movement itself. It is very hard to understand the animal rights ideology through the simple exercise of logic. Because of the increasingly religious nature of the movement, what may appear to be very logical to them, is totally illogical to others.

Before the religious nature of animal rights and its present stage of evolution can be understood, it is necessary to understand a little of its history.

For many years there were a number of groups throughout the U.S. and Europe who protested various practices which involved the use of animals. Some groups protested the practice of dog fights where dogs were placed into a small arena where they fought to the death. Cock fighting, which was a similar practice, was also protested. Most hunters and trappers supported the elimination of such practices and they were soon outlawed.

Still other groups protested the practice of hunting and trapping, but because most of society recognized the value of these activities, these groups were never taken very seriously.

Because they had not yet adopted the terms "animal liberation" or "animal rights" they were described simply as anti-trappers or anti-hunters; or in some instances, because of their fanatical behavior, they were described as "bunny huggers" or simply as "animal lovers."

It wasn't until the mid to late 60's that this relatively obscure, and ill-defined movement, started to take shape. This transformation is fully covered in chapter six.

Through the 70's and early 80's, there were very few indications that the movement had any religious foundations. It is now very apparent that the founders of the new movement were very careful to conceal their religious philosophies, although the answer was always there. All trappers and hunters had to do was ask themselves one simple question. If all the precepts of animal liberation were to be enacted this very moment, what would be the final result? The answer is simple, in fact, it was apparently too simple to recognize . . . we would all be forced into VEGETARIANISM.

Although Henry Salts' book titled "Animal Rights" is presented as a book dedicated to animal liberation, in truth it is a book dedicated to "vegetarianism." Likewise, Peter Singer's book titled "Animal Liberation" is viewed as the "Bible" of animal rights . . . while in reality it is a book that promotes "vegetarianism." People for the Ethical Treatment of Animals (PETA) is recognized as an animal rights group, but their stated purpose is: "To reduce and eventually eliminate the consumption of animals." Vegetarianism. By simply implying one thing, while promoting something totally different, they were able to deceive millions of people.

In fact, neo-vegetarianism (the best name to describe this new religious movement) could be viewed by a psychologist as an almost perfect clinical example of reverse psychology. To understand vegetarianism in general, and neo-vegetarianism specifically, one must reverse the stated goals of the philosophy. When this is done, all their true goals fall into place. Notice that throughout the balance of this chapter how this "ILLUSION" has worked. The failure to recognize the religious aspects of animal rights lies in the fact that most people falsely recognized vegetarianism as THE RESULT of animal rights when in reality it is the cause.

Although most people recognize a "vegetarian" as a person who lives by eating vegetables, fruits and grains, such a description doesn't accurately describe the philosophy of vegetarianism. The fact that the descriptive name "vegetarian" was given to them by people outside the movement, as a way of describing their practice, further suggests that few people understand their philosophy.

A better description of their practice would be that it promotes a diet that is "meat, or flesh-free." Vegetarians don't eat fruits, grains and vegetables simply because they like them, but rather because they abhor the thought of eating meat. This is a very important distinction.

Although this would suggest that vegetarians love animals too much to eat their flesh, and in fact, that is what they imply, just the opposite is true. Vegetarianism is, and has been throughout history, the most self-serving, self-centered philosophy that I can imagine. It is a religious philosophy that offers only benefits for man. In their eyes, there are no negatives.

Even the ancient practice of vegetarianism offered MAN a higher spirituality, and upon his death, a greater heavenly bliss.

The appeal of neo-vegetarianism is that it promises more immediate rewards for its followers. Not only does it offer a superior moral and spiritual nature, it also protects their tender feelings by the promise to eliminate the visual insult of death and suffering in animals, which they suggest, will ultimately lessen the suffering of MAN. They often state that: "If man can learn to love animals, he will also learn to love MAN."

While animal rights organizations spend millions of dollars to stop the death of cows, chickens, ranch mink and game and fur animals, which number into the millions, they have never spent one thin dime to help save endangered species. This very selfish philosophy is best illustrated by one of the patron saints of vegetarianism.

"This is dreadful! Not the suffering and death of animals, but that man is suppressing himself, unnecessarily, the highest spiritual capacity." (4)

Leo Tolstoy.

It is obvious that they feel that it is better for an animal to have never lived than to be required to die at the hands of man. This explains the remark from the lady from New Jersey that I mentioned earlier. I'll repeat her statement; "It's better for animals to become extinct, than to die at the hands of man."

Neo-vegetarianism ultimately benefits only one species ... man.

The neo-vegetarian movement, although not a dominant religious presence in either Europe or America, has become a very pervasive and increasingly militant influence in our societies. Although they are not recognized by most people as a religious movement, it is only because they hide their religious doctrines behind a facade of humanitarian, ethical and health related goals that they are able to deceive the public to their true motives.

Because the ancient practice of vegetarianism was originally founded in the Hindu religion, and the worship of animals, it is recognized in the U.S. as a quasi-religious practice or ritual rather than a religion in and of itself. Today's version of vegetarianism is a hybrid of the ancient practice, and has evolved into a religion that stands alone and separate from its ancient beginnings. This hybrid of the old and new explains why the deception has been so complete.

This new concept perhaps began with the introduction of Darwin's Theory of Evolution. Suddenly, in some people's minds (especially highly educated people who have had extensive exposure to evolutionary theory) the ancient practice of vegetarianism no longer made sense on the basis that it showed reverence for species (animals) that are "incomplete" in their evolution. How can these inferior species be viewed as gods? By virtue of his higher evolution, the highest example of evolution in the known universe, the only true God is MAN. At this point, the true meaning of vegetarianism, which even in its ancient form promised the attainment of higher spiritual growth for MAN, took on new meaning.

Neo-vegetarianism, and the evolutionary theory, complement each other almost tit for tat. The theory of evolution, in their minds, proves that even the physical evolution of man can be changed, and through the manipulation of our evolution, "lions can be made into lambs and wolves into cattle." Thus the very nature of man can be altered from vicious to passive, dominant to subservient, and thus attain a higher, more "God like" image.

"He is blessed who is assured the animal is dying out in him day by day and the divine being established."(5)

Thoreau.

The common statement "you are what you eat" is obviously the first commandment of neo-vegetarianism. In scientific terms, this statement makes no sense. If you eat only vegetables, you don't become a vegetable. But the theory of evolution does suggest that if we eat plant life long enough, we will evolve into a different species. From aggressive lions to passive sheep.

An even greater proof that neo-vegetarianism is a separate entity from the ancient practice of vegetarianism lies in the separation from their basic principles.

The ancient practice of vegetarianism promoted a subservient, non-aggressive and passive nature. In fact, passivism was one of the promised benefits on which the vegetarian practice, or ritual, was founded.

Neo-vegetarianism, under the guise of animal rights, promotes a totally opposite ideology where violence and terrorism is actually encouraged to promote their cause. Practitioners of the ancient form of vegetarianism will ultimately recognize neo-vegetarianism as a perverted form of the practice. Eventually they will have to question whether neo-vegetarianism is producing saints or sinners.

Although Peter Singer is often described as the "Guru of Animal Rights," in reality he should be recognized as a high priest of the neo-vegetarian religion. In his book "Animal Liberation" on page ten he says when speaking for himself and his wife; "we were not especially interested in animals. Neither of us has ever been inordinately fond of dogs, cats or horses in the way that many people are. We didn't love animals."

Although this statement was made in the past tense, nowhere in his book does he suggest that his feelings towards animals has changed. This would seem inconsistent with his image as an animal liberator and in fact is. After the facade of "humane treatment of animals," recognizing animals as our "evolutionary ancestors," "speciesism" and the "health benefits" of vegetarianism are recognized, not as beneficial to animals as most people interpret them, but rather as a higher evolution of human spirituality, the true goal of neo-vegetarianism becomes apparent.

After all, animals will never appreciate, or even understand, at least in human terms, compassion. Nor will they ever feel equal to humans. Equality and compassion describe human characteristics that are never found, and have absolutely no place in the lives of animals.

Neo-vegetarians suggests that only through the abandonment of animals can our spiritual (and according to the laws of evolution) physical evolution be changed, or accelerated, to achieve our full potential as a deity.

To understand this philosophy we can learn from earlier high priests of vegetarianism; Abstinence from flesh food is "a great aid to the evolution of the spirit." (6)

Gandhi.

The advantage of a reform in diet is obviously greater than that of any other. It strikes at the root of evil. (7)

Percy Bysshe Shelly.

The animal rights movement is obviously a battle between two religious philosophies that until now only the neo-vegetarians understood. All of our present shepherd/herd systems are built on the Judeo-Christian ethic, and the new gurus understand, and openly demand, that we must abandon this ethic in favor of animal rights (neo-vegetarianism).

The animal rights groups constantly suggest that animal cruelty (as they see it) is the result of Judeo-Christian teachings which gave man dominion over animals. (Gen. 1:28) And God blessed them, and God said unto them, be fruitful, and multiply, and fill the earth, and subdue it; and have dominion over the fish of the sea, over the fowl of the air and over every living thing that moveth upon the earth.

What does dominion mean? The World Book Dictionary explains; "1. The power or right of governing and controlling; rule; control." This obviously can apply to much more than animals. To accept this teaching demands the acceptance of God's dominion over humans; human dominion over other humans; (human leadership), and finally human dominion over animals. In the neo-vegetarian religion (animal rights) such dominion cannot be tolerated. In effect it is the first step in rebellion against all authority. To start at the bottom of the chain, and return animals into the hands of nature, and thus destroy man's dominion over animals, is the logical first step. "Even if God or nature sides with the killer, the vegetarian is saying: I protest the ways of God and man." (8)

Isaac Bashevis Singer.

"We ... have to recognize that the Judeo-Christian religious tradition is our foe." (9)

Peter Singer.

Because of the present immoral nature of man, which they feel is illustrated by the trappers and hunters predatory nature, the only way we can shed the constraints of government (dominion) is to become the spiritual equivalent of gods. To do this we must sacrifice (abandon) our animals, for the physical evolution and spiritual advancement of man.

This also explains the disregard animal rights leaders often show for the mentally and physically impaired members of human society, whom they often suggest, should be used in replacement of animals for medical research. It's apparent that the neo- vegetarian religion recognizes the fact that these people can never evolve into a position of deity.

The next most logical question must be; If neo-vegetarians recognize MAN as God, why do they protest animal research? After all, medical research is designed to minister to man? Again, human evolution is the answer.

One of the animal rightists' biggest complaints against hunting and trapping is that it interferes with the process of natural selection. In the evolutionary theory, animals evolve into a higher state because only the genetically superior and most adaptable animals in a species are able to survive the ravages of starvation, disease and predation. Because only the survivors pass on their superior genes, while inferior animals die, this will ultimately produce, in their eyes, a stronger, genetically superior species.

This explains their total disregard for the argument that the elimination of hunting and trapping will produce devastating results in the form of starvation, disease and predation for animals. Apparently, they feel it is a positive result.

This also explains why they show little concern for the extinction of whole species. It's obvious that they feel that such results are a normal and positive part of the evolutionary process.

It quickly follows that if they feel that "natural selection" is important to animals, they have to feel that medical research interferes with the "natural selection" of humans. Medical research, and the medical advances it produces, allows the introduction of genetically inferior humans into our collective gene pool. Again, it interferes with the higher physical evolution of man.

Trappers especially have long been confused by the fact that most animal rights advocates, while fighting for the rights of the helpless animal on one hand, (and want to provide the "voice" for those unfortunate creatures who can't defend themselves) on the other hand support free and unfettered abortion of the helpless unborn humans who also cannot defend themselves.

This seems inconsistent with their dedication to end all killing of animals. After all, unborn humans, in their eyes are animals who, they must agree, have no voice in their treatment. This has been viewed as a form of worship of animals, when just the opposite is true.

Abortion can ultimately be used as a form of both natural and artificial selection. As our ability to determine the mental and physical quality of the unborn fetus increases, it will become possible for us to eliminate the inferior examples long before they are able to contaminate our genetic pool.

Many animal rights leaders also condone the practice of euthanasia, and why not? Old people have served their purpose of adding to the gene pool, and are no longer needed.

It appears obvious, that Hitler's desire to build a superior race is shared by other people, even today. As could be expected, the neo-vegetarian movement was founded, and draws virtually all of its support from, those who consider themselves society's elite upper class. This religious ideology is formed on the principle that man is supreme in all of nature, and thus has the intellectual power, and the moral right, to manipulate mankind into his own image of deity. This is the ultimate, and most perverted example of intellectual, social and moral elitism.

"We possess a predatory instinct, which is part of our primitive nature. However, those who have cultivated their spiritual nature are disturbed by the notion that killing for food is justifiable not withstanding our predatory nature." (10)

Thoreau.

Although what he is saying may not be apparent to most people, it is obvious that this is a very "elitist" statement. He is suggesting that those who have cultivated their spiritual nature (vegetarians) are superior. Those of us who have not, are "primitive."

The problem with such a elitist ideology is that although the founders and promoters of such a religious belief may have the giant egos necessary to formulate such an ideology, many of their followers often suffer from an almost total lack of ego.

As in any religious cult, often the first to commit themselves are the emotional cripples. These are people who have trouble fitting into society, or who feel abused and neglected by other humans. Some may feel lonely and depressed, or have lost a friend or loved one and feel abandoned. Such people are often quick to embrace gods (animals) who in their eyes are passive, loving, sinless, loyal and unlike "man" the god, and the Judeo-Christian God, they are non-critical. Animals accept eccentric behavior. They make no distinction between fat and skinny, ugly or beautiful, smart or dumb, young or old. They are not insulted by your speech, your attitude or your personality. More importantly, they do not hold you accountable for your "sins."

Many animal rights followers have openly stated that animals show an un-questioning and un-dying love. They have feelings, and emotions; they are better, in many respects, than the human animal, and have for too long been crucified for the benefit of man! To use them for any purpose, no matter how noble, is immoral. A sin.

It is virtually impossible for people with low self-esteem to look at man in the position of a god, either now, or in some future state of evolution. They are smart enough to see and, because of their situation in life, often dwell on the flaws in man's character.

But, if man is little more than another animal as was suggested by Ms. Newkirk's statement that "A rat is a pig is a dog is a boy," than we are all of one flesh. This suggestion is constantly being presented by virtually every leader in the movement. Peter Singer, in his book "Animal Liberation" page 217 suggests that the eating of flesh is "cannibalism." In the words of another vegetarian; "Life is offered to me on condition of eating beefsteaks . . . but death is better than cannibalism." (11)

George Bernard Shaw.

On this basis, in the minds of some people, only one small step in faith is required to change their worship of one animal, "Man" to the worship of other animals, "the rat OR the pig OR the dog."

Because neo-vegetarian (animal rights) leaders have hidden their true goals of making MAN into gods, it's not hard to understand why most of their followers have chosen the wrong animals, i.e. (non-human) to worship. (The New World Dictionary defines worship as; 1. To pay great honor and respect to: revere, venerate. 2. To consider extremely precious; hold very dear; adore.)

Neo-vegetarians tolerate, and even encourage, animal worship because it produces the desired effect. Ultimately animal worshipers must, if they are true to their beliefs, become vegetarians. As many of these elitist leaders have said, "The end justifies the means."

The appeal of the animal rights religion obviously lies in the fact that it allows for the worship of many different gods. More importantly, it allows each person to shape his god into whatever form, either physically or spiritually, that is wished. It allows for the worship of an elitist's god, "man" or a very subservient god, "animals."

This phenomenon was predicted in the Bible close to 1900 years ago.

(Romans 1:22, 23) Professing themselves to be wise, they become fools, 23: And changed the glory of the incorruptible God into an image made like corruptible man, and birds, and four-footed beasts, and creeping things.

Whether you view this passage as the inspired word of God, or simply the historical observation of one man, recent events suggest that it is a prophesy coming true.

Although it may be very hard for most people in our modern society to accept the idea of animal worship, history records many examples of man's natural tendencies to elevate animals to positions of deity. In ancient Egypt, cats were recognized as gods. To kill a cat, even by accident, was punishable by death. This worship was obviously instigated by the Pharaohs who were themselves worshiped as gods. But the moment the Pharaoh system was destroyed, Egyptian society gave up its worship of cats. It is apparent that they were forced, or more likely deceived, into accepting this religious belief.

In the Bible, book of Exodus, chapter 32, the Israelites gave of their riches (gold) to fashion a god in the image of a calf, and all the tribe of Israel worshiped it. When Moses made them aware of their worship, a portion (the children of Levi) turned from that worship. Again they were deceived into the worship of an animal.

It is apparent that people can be unknowingly led into the worship of animals. As I have stated on numerous occasions throughout this book, I recognized many of the supporters and believers in animals rights to be VICTIMS of the animal rights philosophy. They are no less VICTIMS of the animal rights movement than are those members of the shepherd/herd systems. The tenderness of heart and spirit which these people profess, has been perverted into a hatred for the great Satan . . . hunters, trappers, etc. Their tenderness has evolved or degraded, depending upon your point of view, into an unnatural reverence for animals.

In 1557 and 1558, two of my ancestors, William and Thomas Carman were burned at the stake by the Queen of England because of their Christian beliefs. Another ancestor, John Carman, fled England in 1631 to escape religious persecution, as did many of our American ancestors. It is a sad reality that better than 300 years later, many people of like belief are again facing severe religious persecution for the belief that man has dominion over animals, and that they were placed here for man to nurture, shepherd, and used to provide sustenance for man.

Although some people will argue that a minority religion cannot persecute a majority, it wasn't until animal rights was recognized as a "powerful" movement that their religious philosophies started to surface. This religious persecution is possible only because of their "perceived" power. Also, in the beginning of their movement, only the smaller shepherd/herd systems were persecuted, and it's possible that people who support animal rights, in one form or another, do outnumber the shepherds of these smaller systems.

This neo-vegetarian religion is not asking us to abandon the Judeo-Christian ethic, THEY ARE FORCING US through the manipulation of our government officials; by disrupting our shepherd/ herd systems; by RELIGIOUS indoctrination of our youth; through terrorism, harassment, and emotional blackmail. And they are doing it under the cover of animal rights. When hunters are harassed in the woods, when people are threatened and assaulted in our streets for wearing fur coats, when medical laboratories are looted and destroyed, and trappers are threatened and harassed by animal rights fanatics . . . it is religious persecution.

I defend the right of any man to be an atheist, agnostic, Muslim, Hindu, Catholic, Protestant, neo-vegetarian, etc; or even to worship animals. I defend his right to propagate his belief by every honorable means, but I protest his intrusion into my life and my culture in his efforts to force society to accept, through religious persecution and indoctrination, their brand of morals and religion.

History is full of examples of religious crusades and "holy wars" that destroyed whole cultures and left political systems in ruin. Such conflicts are the result of religious fanaticism gone wild. As long as our society allows the religious indoctrination and persecution to continue, the potential for such a bloody and vicious "Holy war" in the U.S. grows with each new day.

National Institute of Health deputy director William F. Raub says; "The effectiveness of the animal-rights argument is not in its naked form- "a rat is a pig is a dog is a boy." I think that there are few people who find that appealing. The greatest threat, I think, is in the diversity and the masquerade of the message."

In a recent issue of Animals' Agenda, 1988 a leading animal rights magazine, a full page advertisement is carried for Universal Life-The Inner Religion.

The headline in the ad blurts out, "Christ speaks against violations of animals and vegetarianism." The ad contains two messages said to be "transcripts of revelations through the prophets of our time." The ad does not identify the prophets.

In a revelation reportedly given in 1980, Jesus is quoted to have said, "I was no meat-eater . . . meat as food is not necessary for man." WLFA- Trapper. May, 1988 (page 16).

One Los Angeles Times reader put it like this: "It will never be right to slaughter animals on behalf of mankind for any reason . . . if subjects are needed to render accurate knowledge about the workings of the human organism, there is an endless supply. Take the extreme elderly

and senile. They are largely useless and doomed anyway."
(NY Daily News. Aug. 6, 1989).

** Tom Regan, in his 1983 book, The Case for Animal Rights, says; "If abandoning animal research means that there are some things we cannot learn, than so be it . . . we have no basic right . . . not to be harmed by those diseases we are heir to."

The Washingtonian/February 1990. (Page 193)

*** Cleveland Amory, head as a spokesman for The Fund for Animals, at an anti-trapping rally in Lititz, Pennsylvania in October of '83 said; "I hope all trappers make it to heaven, despite their sinful acts inflicted on animals, and find God to be a fox."

**** Author Cleveland Amory, a major spokesperson for the animal rights extremists, has observed that if his son contracted diabetes and required insulin (which comes from a lamb) he would not approve its use. Source. Fur Retailers information council. 9/1/88.

* In a recent article in FORBES magazine, Ingrid Newkirk, founder and leader of PETA, when speaking of her childhood was quoted as saying "It was a desolate, very lonely experience." It scars you for life. After all, you're desperate to get in touch with your parents, but by the time you do go home you really hate and resent them."

** Animal worship has become a clear and present danger to U.S. health and welfare. "So called animal rights groups have launched a campaign of disinformation and political harassment against animal husbandry. (Barron's Feb. 13,1989).

The editors of U.S.A. Today described them as, "A cult of animal worshipers."

CHAPTER 16
THE "SICKNESS" OF VEGETARIANISM

The effects of the disease are complete when they view themselves as "normal" and the rest of society as primitive, barbaric and arrogant.

Although many people today practice vegetarianism for the health benefits it promises, there is no medical proof that a totally meat-free diet will assure you of a long, vigorous and healthy life. Most people fail to recognize the real reasons why vegetarianism is promoted so strongly by disciples of the religion, but the fact that they denounce ALL use of meat must surely provide clear evidence of their motives.

True disciples of vegetarianism do not promote the practice for your heath, and in fact, every indication would suggest they couldn't care less about your physical well being. In virtually all vegetarian literature, the dominant reason given for entering into the practice themselves, is to end the pain and suffering our "abnormal" diet causes to innocent animals

Because most people in our modern society are not tormented by the thought of sitting down to a breakfast of ham and eggs, disciples of vegetarianism will accept and encourage any rationale for "conversion" to their cause.

Peter Singer suggests that because all animals, which include man, can feel pain, we must all be viewed as equal. Fundamental differences; language, moral perceptions and the ability to reason, are not important. Because we are equal, any use of animals whether for food, clothes, sport or companionship, in his eyes, is the moral equivalent to racism.

Although this could be taken to suggest that only people outside the neo-vegetarian religion recognize animals as inferior, one of the patron saints of vegetarianism remarks;

" It is beneath our dignity as human beings to imitate the ways of predatory animals: I hold flesh-food to be unsuited to our species. We err in copying the lower animals if we are superior to it." (12)

Gandhi.

It is obvious that this conflict in reasoning is caused by their worship of different gods, but as could be expected, this willingness to accept any rationale for change has created a great deal of confusion and contradiction within the vegetarian (animal rights) movement.

Famous author, philosopher and vegetarian, Isaac Bashevis Singer, best describes the rationale behind the practice of vegetarianism. He comments:

"Nature is cruel, but we should not contribute to that cruelty. Actually, vegetarianism is a protest against the cruelty of nature." (13)

It is apparent that the neo-vegetarian religion adheres to the philosophy that "the end justifies the means." A person's reasons for becoming a vegetarian are not important, as long as (in their view) it ends the needless suffering of animals.

Because true proponents of vegetarianism enter into the practice because of their suggested concern for the pain and suffering of animals, one step away from animal usage requires another, followed by another, and still another. If you stop eating meat, it's only logical that you stop wearing leather, or eating dairy products, eggs, and even honey.

In vegetarianism, as in many established religions, there are levels of progression. The highest level, or possibly lowest, depending on your view of vegetarianism, is exemplified by the "vegan" society, established in England in 1944.

In his book, "Vegetarianism. A Way of Life." Dudley Giehl described the "Vegans" in this way.

Many vegans also do not use honey. In addition to eliminating all types of animal foodstuffs from their diet, a considerable number of vegans also avoid using non-food animal products, e.g., leather, fur, wool, etc. These practices are based on the ethical philosophy that it is wrong to kill animals or exploit them in any way.

The perversion of this religious philosophy lies in the fact that they can never eliminate, and in fact may actually increase suffering in animals. When animals are left to the hands of nature they die from predation, fighting, accident, starvation or disease. All of these can be considered, in human terms, as cruel and inhumane. Even if society made a total conversion to vegetarianism, it would still require the death of animals by the cutting blades, and under the wheels, of grain combines.

A simple protest against nature, as Isaac Bashevis Singer suggests, contrary to their evolutionary beliefs, cannot change nature.

Because vegetarians are obviously disturbed by the mere thought of suffering in animals, the fact that no matter what they do, animals will continue to suffer, consumes their very souls.

The danger of vegetarianism is that it is a degenerative disease of the human spirit. It demands the regression of man's perception of God, "From an incorruptible God, to corruptible man, and finally to birds, four footed beasts and creeping things." (Romans 1:23) It turns a tender and compassionate heart, into a spirit of radicalism, hate and intolerance. The effects of the disease are complete when they view themselves as "normal" and the rest of society as "primitive, barbaric and arrogant," a description used by Ingrid Newkirk in a 1985 City Paper interview.

Neo-vegetarians often talk about a utopian world where "the lion will lie down with the lamb, where man will live in harmony with nature, where when two animals fight, human beings will intervene," a vision evoked by Ingrid Newkirk. Another proponent of the new religion, Michael W. Fox, advocates "Returning to Eden" in his 1980 book by that title. He further suggests that "Human beings aren't superior to the other animals, we're just different. We need to think not in terms of a hierarchy, but what I call a "holarchy," a seamless web of life."

This hopeless desire for a utopian world free of pain and suffering, destroys their chance of happiness or contentment here on earth, and condemns them to a life of hellish mental torment. And the absolute dedication their Gods demand provides the cause of that torment . . . but never the salvation.

"IT'S BETTER FOR ANIMALS TO DIE AT THE HANDS OF NATURE THAN TO DIE BY THE HANDS OF MAN."

Basic "doctrine" of Animal Rights.

STARVATION.

"WE MUST EDUCATE SOCIETY TO THE CRUELTY, PAIN, AND SUFFERING OF ANIMALS, CAUSED BY MANS EXPLOITATION OF THESE "INNOCENT" CREATURES"

Stated "Goal" of Animal Rights.

CHAPTER 17

THE SHEPHERD/HERD SYSTEMS
THE FUR FARMER

In the long history of farming, which in many cultures dates back many centuries, fur farming is a relatively new industry dating back less than a hundred years.

Fur farming is unique in that it originated in North America, and was brought to its highest level of expertise in the United States.

For many years it was considered impossible to raise wild mink and fox in captivity; both animals were thought to be too high strung and nervous to be raised successfully, or profitably. Both animals are very prone to a number of fatal diseases, as are most wild animals, and very little was known about their breeding habits. But through the dedicated efforts of a small handful of people, who were highly skilled in the science of animal husbandry, the problems were slowly solved, and a new industry was born.

Few people in our modern society can understand or appreciate the obstacles which these pioneers overcame. Mink especially, take a great deal of skill and knowledge to raise successfully, and only those who have patience and a great understanding of animals can do so. There are virtually no fur farmers in the business today who did not serve a long apprenticeship before starting on their own. Those who do start on their own must begin small and slowly build their knowledge with a great deal of advice and help from more experienced farmers.

Fur farming, like all farming endeavors, is very hard work involving long hours of physical labor. Because of the skill needed, even the largest and most successful farmers must personally be involved in the critical aspects of everyday tasks.

The one key to successful fur farming is cleanliness. Mink especially are very susceptible to a whole range of diseases, and it is only through rigid sanitation efforts, and almost constant testing, that a farmer can be sure of the survival of his animals, and ultimately his business. Mink must also be fed a well-balanced diet of perfectly fresh food. Because mink will quickly die after eating even slightly tainted food, great care is taken in food handling. Food that would give a man an upset stomach, will kill a mink.

As a result of this, fur farmers are all highly-skilled animal dietitians, who vary the animals' diet to best serve the animals' needs. During cold months, the fat content is increased to produce more body heat and prepare them for the breeding and whelping season in the spring. During summer and early fall, the diet is also changed so the animal can better cope with the warmer weather. And finally, before pelting season the protein content of the feed is increased to produce a more beautiful and silky fur.

Although many animal rights advocates suggest that this is a waste of good food, that could be better used to feed starving people, (one of the few times they show concern for humans) most of the ingredients that go into mink food are not normally used for human consumption. Mink and fox food is often made from ground calf heads, scraps from salt water fish, dead chicks from hatcheries, cow stomachs and liver, and chicken necks and backs. It's almost an insult when often wealthy animal rights advocates suggest that humans should eat this stuff, but it does make fur animals fat and healthy.

It has been said that there is an inherent cruelty in raising mink in the relatively small cages in which they are housed, and because wild mink maintain large territories, it is unnatural for them to live in close confinement.

Such statements are either totally self serving to promote the idea of animal rights, or stem from total ignorance. Most likely a combination of both. First of all, an animal that is born and raised in a cage neither knows, nor longs for anything different. Secondly, smaller cages facilitate the handling of the mink which is necessary to treat sickness, testing for disease, observation of the animal and breeding. In effect, it insures their health and reproduction.

Although it is true that wild mink usually have fairly large territories in which they live, it is through necessity rather than choice. In the wilds a mink must find its own food, and under the harsh conditions of winter especially it takes a large area to produce enough food for the animal to survive. It is also necessary to regularly patrol their territories to keep out other mink that may intrude on their areas. Male mink especially have large travel routes, but this is a result of their search for females to breed, and even during the non-breeding season they maintain contact with the females in their area.

Ultimately the size of a mink's territory is determined by the amount of natural food supplies available, and much of a wild mink's life involves eating and sleeping, which varies little from the life of a fur farm mink. Although ranch mink have very small nest boxes, the size of such boxes is critical to mink survival. It is, first of all, perfectly natural for a mink to have a very small den even in the wilds. In fact, most wild mink nest in holes and cavities that are much smaller than the nest boxes provided at a mink ranch. Wild mink are relatively small animals with very little body fat to keep them warm. As a result they must have a very small den hole so that their body heat can warm the den. Ranch mink are larger and normally have a heavy layer of fat between the skin and hide which allows for slightly larger nest boxes. But a nest box that is too large would increase the chances of the mink freezing to death on even moderately cold nights.

Another complaint that is often heard is the methods of killing ranch animals. I have personally observed animals being killed in slaughterhouses, at animal shelters, by veterinarians, and by mink ranchers. There is little doubt that the methods of killing fox and mink are just as quick and humane as any other methods I've seen. It should be understood that a mink farmer has only a matter of days to pelt his mink while the fur is at its peak of primness. As a result, a mink rancher must kill what may amount to several thousand mink in a matter of a few days' time. To do this, the mink must be killed very quickly. Because mink are handled often they are not unduly frightened when lifted from their cages. On most mink ranches they are then placed in a small box where they are asphyxiated with carbon monoxide gas, from the exhaust from a small gasoline motor which is cooled so the animal isn't overheated. We have all heard of people being overcome with exhaust fumes without even knowing it, so it is the most humane death possible.

Ranch foxes in other countries are often electrocuted, which doctors have told me is so instantaneous that the fox is dead before he can feel pain. I have also talked to people who have been knocked unconscious from electricity, and they all agree that it happened so quickly that there was no sensation of pain whatsoever. Most of the ranched foxes in the U.S. are killed with a painless injection in exactly the way as pets are euthanized by the veterinarians.

Many people do not realize that all wild mink are light brown to almost black in color, and except for the very rare albino mink, there was virtually no variation from this basic dark color. But, deep in the genes of these wild mink were found a number of color variations, and soon mink ranchers were producing pastels, buffs and other color variations.

Just as the original farmers produced different variations of cattle, and different breeds of dogs, these breeders produced as many variations that the mink's genetic makeup had to offer.

Animal rights groups use the argument that ranch mink are raised for only one reason . . . to satisfy women's vanity. In fact, fur farming was an industry born through necessity.

During the 1920's, the fur industry was going through one of its boom stages, and fur coats were all the rage. At the time, virtually all furs were taken from the wilds, and the demand for furs far outstripped the supply. The demand was so great that the populations of some fur animals was becoming depleted. Soon the cycle of fashion turned, and no lasting damage was done. But, many of the leaders in the fur industry recognized the fact that with a growing world population of humans, the next fur boom could create a market for furs that even abundant wildlife populations couldn't supply. Although seasons on wild furbearers were set to control the harvest of wild fur, if the demand for furs become great enough, and their price high enough, there could be a danger of poaching in the poorer rural areas of the country, which could permanently damage furbearer populations. The establishment and growth of fur farming eliminated this fear, and helped to stabilize the fur industry, and eliminated the chance of wild fur becoming so valuable that it would present a danger to our wild furbearing herds. It is another example of one herd protecting another.

CHAPTER 18
THE ROLE OF THE HUNTER

Because a relatively small group of men, in a society that seemingly had little concern about wild animals, and in many cases considered them pest and predators, recognized them as treasures, a new and radically different shepherd/system was born.

For thousands of years mankind was a hunter out of necessity, but the life of the nomadic hunter was too dependent upon the whims of nature, often resulting in a life of either feast or famine.

In a nature yet untouched by man, animals often went through extreme population cycles. Most animals are so susceptible to disease and overpopulation, that relatively short periods of high animal populations usually caused massive die-offs from disease and starvation. This often produced prolonged periods of very low populations, while the disease ran its full course, or until the habitat was able to rejuvenate itself enough for a new cycle to start.

During periods of high animal populations the hunter lived a life of plenty, but during low cycles the hunter and his band often suffered from famine.

Because of man's superior intelligence, he soon broke the bonds forced by nature, and started to domesticate animals so that he could control and manage the herd. Suddenly he was no longer totally dependent on the cycles of nature. Even during periods of extreme drought he could nurture the herd and assure its survival, and in turn, increase the chances of survival for his family.

In a relatively short time, man no longer needed to be a hunter, although fortunately, he retained his taste for wild meat, and the thrill of the hunt.

For many years wild game was only valued as a free source of food, and virtually anyone could kill game without restriction. As our human population expanded, this unrestricted pressure on wildlife grew, and with the corresponding loss of wildlife habitat caused by the farmer's plow, many animal species were being pushed close to extinction.

Someone had to take on the responsibility of protecting and managing the herd. At that point something happened that is unique in man's history. Because a relatively small group of men, in a society that seemingly had little concern about wild animals, and in many cases considered them pests and predators, recognized our wild animals as treasures, a new and radically different shepherd/ herd system was born.

Most people today do not appreciate the obstacles these men had to overcome in their early efforts to shepherd the wild animal herds. Society recognized animals as community property, and when these men started placing restrictions on the slaughter of these animals they faced tremendous resistance. Unlike the European system in which the kings retained ownership of the game animals, this new system, which allowed an equal sharing of our animal resources, was what made the system work so successfully. In this system, anyone could harvest wildlife, as long as people followed the rules of the new system. It is this system of shared resources and shared responsibility for these resources, that survives to this day. Those who didn't want a share in the resource, did not have to share the responsibility of shepherding the herd.

So foreign is this system of shared ownership of our animals to the European system, where only the very rich, or people of royal blood, are able to follow the sport of hunting, that they fail to understand or accept our system even to this day. It is interesting that a number of people who formulated the animal rights philosophy were raised under the European system and, as their philosophy indicates, still adhere to the idea that only the elite of society should decide the fate of animals.

The first thing that was established in this new shepherd/ herd system was carefully regulated harvesting periods. These men recognized the danger of harvesting animals during their breeding season, and during the season when animals raise their young. It was also understood that the best time for harvesting animals was just prior to winter when animal populations were at their peak, and many of the animals harvested at this time would not survive the following winter, and the cropping of these excess animals helped assure the survival of the remaining animals.

To do this, the hunter had to set up systems to police his own ranks. Game laws were enacted and game commissions were set up to train and manage this self-imposed police force. In time these game commissions expanded into more scientific methods for both the monitoring and management of the herds. College courses were developed to train these wildlife experts, in what has become a very advanced and technical system of management needed to protect and manage wildlife against the inroads of man.

So successful have hunters been at nurturing the herd and controlling its populations, that widespread disease and starvation is almost unheard of in most big game species. Although this has been a source of great pride for the hunter, most people no longer realize the amount of suffering that would be caused if these good shepherds were forced to abandon their herds. Only people who have seen such animals in the advanced stages of disease and starvation can appreciate the agony and suffering they must endure.

Although many people complain today of not having a voice in the matters of game animals they must realize also that they never had to carry the burden of shepherding the herds. After billions of the hunters' dollars have been spent in the shepherding of the herd, and millions of volunteer man hours have been spent by sportsmen, it seems ridiculous that a small group of people, who never shared that responsibility, now feel that they deserve to become THE voice in the future of wildlife.

In fact, this idea is so ridiculous, that many sportsmen do not appreciate the real danger presented by these people. Hunters do not recognize the fact that a growing number of people in our modern society do not understand or appreciate the service they have rendered to wildlife, and as a result are increasingly susceptible to the animal rights propaganda. Furthermore, hunters do not recognize the fact that in the near future they face a major power struggle, that unless taken very seriously, could seriously cripple if not totally destroy their shepherd/herd system.

Unlike the fur industry, where survival is dependent on a product of the industry, hunters are the consumers of the fruits of their labor. As a result, the attack on the sport of hunting is recognized by hunters as different and less effective. Hunters also recognize the fact that the trappers shepherd/herd system is smaller, and as a result doesn't have the strength to resist the attack against them, whereas they consider the hunters' shepherd/herd system too powerful and important to be destroyed. It is this false sense of security that could lead to the crippling and even the fall of their system.

Hunters must understand that their credibility as shepherds of the herd has been and will continue to be, seriously eroded in the collective mind of society. The animal rights groups have already been very effective at portraying hunters as careless, trigger happy slobs. This has been the theme of numerous T.V. specials starting with the CBS special "The Guns of Autumn." In the months of February and March, 1990, two programs were aired on national T.V. which continued to attack the credibility of hunters. On N.B.C.'s Geraldo show, hunters were accused of carelessly shooting at people's homes resulting in the death of a young child. Although no proof was given to establish the fact that it was a hunter's bullet that killed the child, because it was hunting season, hunters were blamed. A short time later, on ABC's 20/20, a woman was shown teaching her children to "hit the ground" at the report of the hunter's rifle. We are all being blamed for the sins of the few.

What is significant about this is that during that same period of time virtually nothing was aired on national T.V. about the almost daily gun battles on our city streets between drug dealers and rival gangs. Gun battles that spray bullets into homes, endangering and even killing innocent people.

It is also an amazing fact that more money, and a far more effective attack is being made against the image of hunters and trappers than drug dealers. While drug dealers are often portrayed as poor people, making money the only way they know how, hunters and trappers are portrayed as vicious, gun toting, destroyers of innocent creatures. There is presently more literature in our schools, on our T.V., and in our magazines, which is designed to turn our children against hunters and trappers as individuals, than there is against drug pushers.

While the entertainment industry exerts tremendous peer pressure to stop the sale of fur, they turn their face aside from drug use. It is not unreasonable to assume that many of the people in the entertainment industry, who have come out in open opposition to hunting and trapping, either currently use drugs, or have used drugs in the past, and thus support an industry that is destroying our future.

Long before hunting is totally prohibited, it will be weighed down with restrictions designed to destroy the freedom now enjoyed by hunters.

As the non-hunting public is turned against hunters, more and more land will be restricted from hunting. Hunters will have to band together and lease land on which to hunt, which has already started in many areas of the country. The cost of leasing such land will quickly rise, and in the not too distant future, we could have a European-type system in which only the wealthy will be able to hunt.

Animal rights groups are constantly introducing legislation that would restrict, and even eliminate, hunting on public property. Presently, they are demanding that they be represented on game management boards, and also that they be given a voice in the police forces which hunters have put into force to police their own ranks. If they are successful, they will have the power to first disrupt, and ultimately destroy those systems.

As in all the other shepherd/ herd systems, the lowest

level of society will be the ones to suffer first, and to suffer the most.

There is little doubt that the biggest problem hunters face is the smearing of the hunters' image by the media elite. They have no way of understanding what motivates a hunter. Nor will they ever know the peace of mind and spirit the hunter feels as he sits alone on a deer stand, deep in the woods, with only the sound of a gentle breeze blowing through the evergreens.They will never know the shared love of the outdoors that grows between a hunter and his son, that will live with both until the day they die.

The media elite recognize the "hunter" instinct as an aberration in human behavior that must be exposed and ridiculed, with the hope that "normal" society will reject and condemn it.

It is often far too easy to oppose something you don't understand, and it is even easier to destroy something that a small group of moral and intellectual elitists has portrayed as cruel to animals, and dangerous to innocent people.

Unlike the Europeans who for centuries were unable to hunt because the game was owned by royalty, our forefathers recognized our wildlife as property of the people, and anyone who wished to hunt game in this new world was able to.

Some of our greatest war heroes were hunters who honed the skill with the hunting rifle. Audie Murphy, the most decorated soldier of World War II, as a young man, helped feed his poor family by hunting rabbits. Sergeant York, one of our most famous Congressional Metal of Honor recipients was a very proficient turkey hunter in his native hills of Tennessee, and used that skill to trick the enemy, a fact that is well-documented in both movies and literature.

To many people in rural America, hunting is a traditional way of life. Most hunters will fight violently to keep that tradition alive, but it's important for them to realize that they cannot rest on their laurels. Like those far-sighted men who founded the hunter's shepherd/ herd system, we must recognize the danger to our personal futures and the future of our herds, and face that danger head on. We have worked too hard, and have too much to lose not only as hunters, but as a nation, to allow our future to be dictated by others.

The questions that the animal rights groups cannot, and will not answer, is what will happen to our herds if the shepherds are destroyed ? How will the farmers keep the deer from eating their crops; what will stop the carnage on our highways caused by collisions between automobiles and deer caused by overpopulation; how do they plan to control diseases in our herds or the massive die-offs caused by lack of harvest? Although the animal rights groups, and the media elite, will not answer these questions, we must continue asking them. Only then will the public start to understand that they are being asked to place the future of their wildlife into the hands of people who only know how to destroy the present system, and have no plans to build another system to take its place.

CHAPTER 19
THE ROLE OF THE TRAPPER

In the Holy Bible, Book of Genesis 2:21 it says, "For Adam also and for his wife did the Lord God make coats of skins, and clothed them."

Whether you believe in the Bible, or in the theory of evolution, everyone must agree that the first clothing to adorn our ancient ancestors was made from the skins of animals.

There are few things in man's history that have captured his fancy more than the beauty of furs. New lands were conquered, great fortunes were made and more than a few woman's favors were bought, with the pelts of animals.

Although there are millions of people in our modern society who have never see a live muskrat, mink or otter in the wilds, they have only to go to an airport or shopping mall in the middle of winter to see the beauty of their fur. In fact most people would never appreciate the beauty of these animals, or even know that they existed as a species, without seeing their beauty in the form of a fur coat.

For years the animal rights groups have worked diligently to destroy the fur industry with very limited success. Although they were able to outlaw the steel trap in Florida and Rhode Island, states of little importance to the fur industry, and in New Jersey because it is a largely urbanized state, for years their plea for a ban on trapping fell largely on deaf ears.

Finally after they realized that they couldn't legislate their morality, they came up with a more devious plan. If they couldn't get the American people to reject the trapping industry, they would attempt to destroy its markets. Since that time they have used every method possible to present the fur coat as the symbol of everything that is sick and perverted in our society.

Suddenly, they had an audience tailor-made for their message. Gone were the biologists and wildlife experts who could justify the need for trapping; gone were the faces of trappers who fought so desperately for their future; gone were the farmers and ranchers asking how they could protect their cattle and sheep.

Now, instead of having to argue their case to politicians and the American people, they found a virtually uncontested forum. They found an audience that did not know, or even care to know, anything about wild animals. An audience that had no way of knowing the consequences that would result from a ban on trapping, to see the death and destruction it would cause to animals, or the hardships it would cause for men.

Almost overnight they had movie and T.V. stars, politicians, artists and writers clamoring to join the new "moral" cause.

For years, politicians have resisted the call to ban trapping because the true experts in wildlife have testified that trapping was a necessary part of wildlife management, and that the elimination of trapping would result in untold suffering in animals, and destruction of valuable wildlife habitat. They were told that if trapping were to cease tomorrow, not one second of suffering would be eliminated in wildlife; and they understood.

Time and again these arguments stymied the efforts of the animal rights movement, and their efforts were almost ground to a halt. In the face of all this, the one argument that is presently being swallowed by the American people is that trapping is unnecessary, and until the American people realize that they are being played for fools, and are being asked to sacrifice something that they do not need to sacrifice, the power the animal rights leaders are seeking, will continue to grow. The sacrifices the American people will be asked to make will become greater, and the burden for much of this will fall on the shoulders of hunters, trappers and livestock farmers.

The biggest danger that would be caused by a ban on trapping will ultimately be on the animals themselves. The one visible symbol of trapping is the fur coat. Without the mink, fox, coyote and beaver coat, most people wouldn't even know these animals exist. Out of sight, out of mind. Many of these animals could, and probably will, be pushed close to extinction and no one will know, or care. That is when the new morality of animal rights will bear the fruits of its perversion.

Although many trappers follow the trapline for the physical and spiritual health it provides, trapping is hard, tiring and often frustrating work. Its financial rewards are very limited, but for many Americans it's a way to make extra money to pay bills, buy Christmas gifts and finance a rare vacation with the family. Although there are trappers from almost every walk of life, it is not normally a sport or business that appeals to the wealthy people of our society.

To become an effective and skillful trapper requires years of experience and dedication to the business. Most animals don't rush to get into your traps, as many would have you believe. It is because of this that the tricks of the trade are often passed down from one generation to another. In many rural families it has become a traditional method of supplementing their often meager incomes.

Although trappers have been portrayed as vicious, sadistic monsters, who revel in the killing of animals, I have yet to meet one who professed a desire to kill anything. As one trapper once told me; "If I liked killing animals, I'd get a job killing animals in a slaughterhouse, or the local S.P.C.A." I have yet to meet a trapper who held either job.

How then do they justify the killing of animals? First of all, far better than half of the animals taken by trappers quickly die by drowning, which is a very merciful death by most standards, or are killed almost instantly in killer traps. The balance are taken in steel traps that hold the animal by the foot for what is normally a matter of hours, before the trapper kills them, usually by shooting them in the head with small caliber rifle or revolver bullet.

The use of the steel jawed trap has been presented by the animal rights groups as the ultimate symbol of what they view is the cruelty of trapping. As a result a great deal of mysticism has surrounded what is in truth a very efficient and very humane tool.

Possibly the biggest problem in defending the steel-jawed trap can be traced to the fact that it is made in a whole multitude of sizes ranging from large enough to hold a six hundred pound bear, to a trap small enough to catch a four ounce weasel. Although trappers select the smallest trap size possible for each species of animals, if for no other reason than the fact that the smaller traps are less costly, protesters of the trap like to suggest just the opposite. Few anti-trap hearings are complete without the appearance of a large bear trap, its jaws lined with teeth, presented as the example of all traps when in fact such traps have long been outlawed, by trappers themselves, in virtually every state. Not because they are inhumane to animals, but because they pose a threat to humans.

The animal rights group "Friends of Animals" has been the most successful at portraying the use of huge traps for trapping of relatively small animals. FoA has made millions of dollars, and gained a great deal of support, by using a picture of a dead coon, that many experts recognize as a road killed coon, with a huge trap on its foot. This photo has been so successful as a fund raising tool for FoA that it has become the most familiar example of animal rights propaganda.

It is no doubt because of such advertising that many people believe most traps are capable of catching and holding humans and especially small children. However, legal-sized traps are incapable of closing over the foot of anything more than infant. In the two hundred year history of trapping there has never been one instance of a child becoming accidentally caught and seriously injured in a steel trap.

The final, and most crucial argument surrounding the steel jawed trap is its perceived potential to inflict great harm to animals resulting in severe pain and suffering. Opponents of the steel trap suggest that it clamps on an animal's foot with bone crushing force which would seem to make it very dangerous to handle by the trapper himself. It's important to consider that there are no safety clamps or devices to prevent the trapper from becoming caught from time to time when setting traps. In fact, I personally have been a trapper for close to forty years, and have accidentally had my fingers caught in traps thousands of times, yet like most trappers, who range from nine years old to eighty, my hands are without blemish from such accidents.

The biggest problem trappers face is the irresponsibility of pet owners. In very rare instances, stray or unsupervised dogs wander into areas where they do not belong and become caught in traps. If such dogs are well disciplined and are accustomed to a leash or chain, they quickly settle down and wait for the trapper to release them. The problems come from dogs that have never been chained. They react just as any dog does when first chained; they fight often violently causing themselves slight damage. Still other dogs have their foot seriously damaged by well meaning people who find the dog in the trap and try to release them. Still other dogs are abandoned by their owners in rural areas (a very common occurrence in some areas) where they invariably wander around until caught in a trap. Because they are lost and bewildered, they often fight the trap resulting in a slight injury to their feet.

Although animal rights sympathizers blow these isolated cases far out of proportion in an obvious effort to shed a negative light on trapping, the general public seldom understands that tens of thousands more of these unsupervised dogs end up under the wheels of cars and eighteen wheelers than are ever caught in traps. "When a dog is caught in a trap it is just as much an accident." The only difference is that when a dog is caught accidentally in a trap, the owner can shift the responsibility of the dog's injury on the trapper rather than rightfully shoulder that responsibility themselves. When people scream about their dogs getting injured in traps, they are really denying their lack of responsibility in not supervising their pets.

It should be understood that virtually all trappers get

permission from the landowner to set their traps on their land. Dogs that wander onto that land are not the responsibility of the landowner or the trapper. The time is long overdue for pet owners to be held responsible for their wards. "It's 11:00 o'clock. Do you know where your pets are?"

I can only add that after over thirty five years of extensive trapping I have never caught a dog that was permanently injured.

In reality the steel jawed trap is not the real issue. Although animal rights groups have portrayed it as a symbol of all that is evil about the fur industry, it does not explain why they feel an obligation to try destroying other segments of the fur industry. The fur seal doesn't even have legs which they can stick into traps. Ranch mink and fox never come in contact with traps. The real motive behind the animal rights movement is destruction of the whole shepherd-herd system and they will work hard to portray our systems, and any instrument we use in our system, in as negative a way as possible.

Although most trappers voice their displeasure of killing animals, most have seen the pain and suffering these animals must endure as a result of starvation and disease. From the time animals are taken from traps, until their furs are made into a fur coat, most of those animals would have suffered and died from natural causes anyway.

Life in nature is seldom easy. Wild animals often become old very quickly. Compared to the pampered life of people's pets, wild animals must often spend long hours of hunting to find a meal. They often have to endure extreme weather conditions, and competition from other animals. Any accident that causes a broken bone, or severe laceration must be endured until it heals or until the animals die. As the animals get older, their reflexes slow, and their teeth become dull. If they survive long enough, they will slowly die of starvation.

Periodic outbreaks of disease kill most animals long before they reach old age. Each year virtually millions of foxes die of the dreadful disease of mange, which is caused by a small parasitic mite that burrows into the skin causing severe itching. As these mange mites reproduce, they ultimately cover every inch of the animal's body, causing the animal to scratch and dig until its body is covered with a mass of weeping sores and scabs. Finally, after approximately two months of intense agony, the fox dies of starvation, infection or exposure. This is a very sad, horrible and wasteful death.

It was better than thirty years ago, when I was seventeen years old, that I saw my first fox in the advanced stages of mange, and it had a very profound effect on me.

I have always had a great interest in the red fox, and personally feel that he is one of our most beautiful furbearers. Although they do have a strong "skunk like" odor about them, to me it is not at all offensive. As I got to know more about them and developed a great respect for them, I found myself questioning whether I wanted to continue trapping them as I had for a number of years. I found myself falling into the trap that many animal rights people find themselves. I was beginning to look for human characteristic in the fox, and when in such a frame of mind, it is something that is very easy to do.

Fortunately, I continued to trap foxes in spite of my reservations. One early fall morning, as I entered a small pasture field, I saw something caught in my trap close to a hundred yards away. I didn't recognize it as a fox, and as I approached closer I began to wonder what kind of creature I had caught. As I approached to within twenty five yards, the wind assaulted my nostrils with the terrible stench of rotted flesh that was obviously coming from the animal in my trap. As I walked up to the animal, I was shocked to realize that it was a fox. Never in my life have I felt so much compassion for an animal as I did for this poor unfortunate creature. He stood there with his head hung down, and his body shivered from the early morning chill. He was caught in my trap, but had not moved it from it's original position. All that remained of his beautiful fur was a small strip down his back bone that he had been unable to reach. The rest of his body was covered with dry crusted scabs and weeping sores. His muzzle and legs were swollen to double their normal size, and his eyes were swollen to mere slits. The putrid stench that rose from this animal almost turned my stomach.

I quickly put the poor animal out of his misery, and took him home in the hopes my father would know what had happened to him. Before my dad would answer any questions, he made me build a fire well away from the house, burn the fox, and bury the remains. He than explained that the fox was suffering from mange and that all our pets, livestock, as well as humans were susceptible. He also explained that this was just one of the things that commonly happen to animals in the wilds, and is nature's way of controlling animal populations.

I suddenly understood, that if I quit trapping fox this is what I would be saving them for. Hours, days and months of intense suffering far greater than they could ever experience in a trap. I decided that moment that it is better for the fox to hang from a woman's shoulders than experience the agonies that nature has in store for them. Since that time I have seen many such foxes in the advanced stages of mange, and each time my heart goes out to them.

Still other diseases that produce intense suffering are distemper in fox, bobcats, and coon; Parvo virus in all canines; Aleutian disease in mink; Tularemia in muskrats and beaver; and rabies in all animals. Each year millions of animals in the U.S. alone die prolonged and painful deaths by these and many other diseases.

Although disease is very prevalent in most animal species, the danger to the survival of the species is limited, as long as the populations are kept in check through careful harvest. The greatest devastation to an animal population is possible only if there is close contact between animals which serves to spread the disease. By harvesting animals in the fall and early winter, when their populations are at their peak, an outbreak of disease is less likely to devastate the population. Fur is prime at those times, so those animals are not wasted.

Trapping is an amazingly efficient and effective method

of managing and controlling the herd. Because of the high cost of traps and equipment, and the added cost of operating a trapline, it is almost impossible for the trapper to over-trap or seriously deplete the animals on his trapline, due to the economics of the situation. Once a trapper harvests the excess animals in a given area the laws of diminishing returns force him to abandon the area for a more productive one, leaving an abundant supply of breeding stock.

Also, trapping doesn't have to be a wide-spread activity in order to produce desirable results for animal populations. Once a trapper harvests the animals out of a block of land, it becomes open territory for animals from surrounding areas that will migrate into these harvested areas almost immediately. This helps relieve possible overcrowding and stress on food supplies in surrounding areas. A trapper could trap as small as ten percent of a muskrat marsh, and by so doing increase the chances of survival for the animals in the other ninety percent.

In effect, the trapper serves to disperse the animal population resulting in less contact between animals, thus lessening the spread of disease.

Nothing makes a trapper more angry than to hear an animal rights fanatic suggest that it's fine for an animal to die naturally, as long as man isn't involved. To suggest that death at the hands of Mother Nature is more morally right, implies that Mother Nature is some kind of goddess to which we should sacrifice our animals.

Trappers recognize two simple facts. Nature produces in abundance. A pair of breeding foxes can easily produce twenty five pups in their lifetime, yet they only need to produce two pups to reproduce themselves. Those twenty three extra pups are the abundance. When they reach maturity, they will either be harvested, or die slowly at the hands of Mother Nature. If Mother Nature is a goddess who wants us to sacrifice our animals, she is a wasteful deity.

The second thing trappers recognize is that the failure to harvest this abundance is a tragic waste of a treasure that the true God gave us to use six thousand years ago, and has never taken away, either by command or substance.

CHAPTER 20
THE FINAL CHAPTER?
THE LIVESTOCK FARMER AND RANCHER

"The liberation of animal life," says George Cave, president of the New York abolitionist group Trans-species Unlimited, "can only be achieved through the overthrow of existing power structures." (14)

(Replace "animal life" with "the masses" and he would be quoting Lenin.)

Some of the greatest victories in the history of warfare were achieved through the element of surprise. If you can lull your enemy into a false sense of security, or trick them into thinking that an attack isn't imminent, their lack of defenses leaves them open to defeat.

The animal rights groups, by attacking trapping and the fur industry first, accomplish four things that are necessary for success in battle. First, they are attacking the weakest link in the shepherd/herd system. Secondly, they lull the main enemy forces into thinking that their main objective is to end the "cruelty" of hunting and trapping. Thirdly, because they have tricked the main forces into a sense of security, they fail to re-enforce and support their weakest defenses. And fourth, by destroying one part of the shepherd/herd system they weaken the whole system.

They have already accomplished the first three goals, and are well on their way to victory on the last. But, the real giant of the shepherd/herd system continues to sleep.

The animal rights organization, People for the Ethical Treatment of Animals (PETA) states as their primary objective "to reduce and eventually eliminate the consumption of animals."

When you realize that the products of the fur trade are not "consumed," and that hunting produces only a negligible part of the food consumed by Americans, it becomes obvious that their ultimate goal is to destroy the livestock farmer and rancher.

Although the livestock industry is seeing the first warning signs of the impending attack on their industry, the idea seems so ridiculous and illogical that they apparently can't comprehend the danger their industry faces.

This is very predictable. For years, trappers were so secure in the knowledge that they held an important position in the management of wildlife that it was years before they understood the danger they faced.

One of the greatest dangers we face is the erosion in our faith in all parts of the shepherd/herd systems. Almost from the inception of the modern animal rights movement in the U.S., hunters and trappers understood that it was a mistake to ask farmers' wives for permission to trap on their property. As the animal rights movement grew, with increasing frequency farmer's wives objected to the practice of hunting or trapping. Once the wife refused permission, the farmer seldom overruled her. Because the average farmers wife reads more books and magazines, and watches more television than her husband, she was exposed to more animal rights propaganda. Numerous anti-trapping and anti-hunting articles have been published in woman's magazines which presented a very negative view of these activities. Such articles were designed to appeal to women's emotions, and apparently were very effective.

So effective, in fact, that over the last several years more and more farmers themselves are refusing hunters and trappers access to their lands. The amount of land that is posted against hunting is increasing at an alarming rate in some areas.

As the animal rights propaganda becomes more pervasive, even farmers themselves have started to turn against these activities, and when asked why, they describe trapping as "cruel" and hunters as "slobs." It's apparent that even members within the shepherd/herd system are becoming victims of the very propaganda that will ultimately be turned against them.

The immediate danger of this is that as farmland becomes closed to trapping and hunting, these shepherd/herd systems are weakened, and the negative image of these activities increases. It's obvious that the animal rights zealots are working very hard to destroy our systems from within as well as from without.

I realize that many livestock farmers and ranchers reading this book will conclude, at this point, that I will say and do anything to defend my sport and industry . . . and they are right! I will do anything that I feel is morally right to defend hunting and trapping. But remember, soon you too will be accused of defending YOUR vested interests. You too will be accused of having the blood of innocent creatures on your hands. You too will be labeled as a cruel, vicious and an uncaring example of our primitive past . . . in fact, you already are.

Go to the library and read Peter Singers book, "Animal Liberation" and you will see what the animal rights people think about YOU. You will quickly realize that YOU are the ultimate prize ... YOU are their ultimate victim.

In recent years, I've been forced to ask myself a question. Could I give up trapping and hunting? My answer is yes. They are not my gods. I have even decided that I could continue to be happy without my sport or profession. But these are not the questions we must ask ourselves. The real questions are; are we willing to allow a small group of moral and intellectual elitists, if not decide, at least meddle in our futures? Should we allow them to paint a picture in the mind's eye of the public that shows hunters, trappers and farmers as vicious, cruel monsters that revel in the suffering of animals? Most importantly, are we willing to sacrifice our sport and our industries to feed a perverted religious philosophy? My answer to these questions is NO. What is your answer?

These groups understand that the dismantling of our livestock systems will involve a very long and protracted struggle that has only just begun. But their attack against other shepherd/herd systems, and their present intrusion into the farming industry, gives us ample warning as to what their strategy has been, and no doubt will continue to be, in their efforts to force their vegetarian goals on the American public.

Although, these groups propose vegetarianism as the ultimate goal for their movement, they recognize it as being too radical a proposal for the public to accept at this time. Instead, they have decided to wreck the present livestock systems, and by so doing, force their vegetarian lifestyle onto the public. They obviously feel so secure in their dedication and religious faith in vegetarianism that they expect people who are initially forced into vegetarianism to embrace the concept once exposed.

They are also very devious in their efforts to portray our animal products as unhealthy and dangerous to human health. We can be sure that there will be a continued effort by animal rights groups to scare the public, by what they view as the contamination of our meat and dairy products by antibiotics, growth hormones, feed supplements, etc. Again, people SCARED into a vegetarian lifestyle.

"A dead cow or sheep lying in a pasture is recognized as carrion. The same sort of a carcass dressed and hung up in a butcher's stall passes as food." (15)

John Harvey Kellogg M.D.

As in all other shepherd/herd systems, the animal rights groups first try to portray the shepherd in a very unfavorable light. Where possible, they try to portray him as cruel and uncaring, and label most, if not all, his activities as unnecessary.

One national animal rights organization, reporting a $4.3 million net worth from 1983 to 1986, calls for a ban on bacon and eggs, labeling the dish, "Breakfast of Cruelty." More and more we are seeing newspaper and magazine articles promoting the health benefits of vegetarianism. Another tactic, designed to win media attention is to spray paint McDonald's restaurants with "McDeath."

Livestock farmers must realize that this has a cumulative effect on consumers. People who become forced into a vegetarian lifestyle because of their perception that meat is dangerous to their health, and is obtained through cruel and inhumane methods, often become the best disciples for the cause.

Livestock farmers must realize that these people are moral elitists, and are so dedicated to their moral cause that they recognize no restrictions or limitations in achieving their ends.

It must be understood that even minor demands from these groups can have major effects on the livestock industry. It is obvious that their first goal is to place restrictions on livestock farming that will cause a rise in the cost of producing meat, dairy, and poultry products. By demanding more open housing; the end to the more obvious examples of factory farming; more humane means of transportation; etc. they can in effect, raise the cost of meat enough to virtually eliminate its use in thousands of lower income households. In a true sense, a degree of forced vegetarianism. By slowly increasing their demands, and simultaneously eliminating our markets, they weaken our system.

Farmers must not be deceived into thinking that higher prices for their products is a positive result of the animal rights movement, because ultimately those higher prices will be overpowered by the cost of keeping up to the restrictions that animal rights will continue to heap upon them.

All of this has the effect of heaping more responsibilities, costs and restrictions on livestock farmers which erodes their strength and destroys their markets.

Presently the animal rights groups suggest that their greatest objections to modern farming practices are early cow-calf separation, veal farming and what they describe as the practice of factory farming.

When it's understood that virtually all modern farm practices could come under their description of factory farming, their potential for mischief and intrusion into the livestock industry knows almost no limits.

It is imperative that livestock farmers become more aware, and possibly even involved in the fight to save trapping and hunting. Only than will they understand, and will be better able to prepare themselves for the increased attack against their own industries that is sure to come.

There is absolutely no reason why each separate part of the shepherd/herd system should fight alone. Just as the animal rights groups fight under the same banner, each segment of the shepherd/herd system should combine their strength to protect "shepherd rights." "United we stand, divided we fall."

CHAPTER 21
MAN--THE ENDANGERED SPECIES ?

No better example of man's contempt for abundance can be illustrated than through his new philosophy concerning human life.

Throughout the Bible, it was recognized that man's greatest blessings were his children, followed by his land and his livestock. Like every other living mammal, man's most important responsibility, after reproduction, was the nurturing of his young. But, to receive and maintain the treasures of a large, strong and healthy family, the first blessing he had to receive was a large herd of livestock, and the land to keep his herds.

Of all the comparisons that can be made; reproduction, nurturing of young and the importance of the herd, are the ultimate examples of the shared nature of man and animal.

In the animal kingdom, there is no greater, more undeniable urge than the need for reproduction. It is one of the few times when animals of the same species have been known to fight and kill for the chance to reproduce themselves as individuals.

This is followed by a period of nurturing the young, a responsibility so deeply rooted in the nature of most animals, that the sacrifice of the mother to save her young in the face of danger is a normal, and in some cases, expected response.

But, upon maturity, the offspring are shoved from the nest, to build a new family, a new nest.

Finally, the ultimate survival of one species, is totally dependent on the survival of another. The predator cannot survive without his prey, and the prey cannot survive without the predator. Man long recognized his need for the herd.

Throughout human history we shared these realities with animals, but, through the power of our intellect, we have started the process of separating ourselves from this basic behavior.

The first step in this separation started the moment man decided that the human animal had become too abundant. In reality, it was a very easy step to make. Man is so prolific and adaptable that our sheer numbers threaten to overpower the ability of the environment to sustain us. Our wastes gobble up our lands, foul the air we breath and the water we drink.

Although we could solve our environmental problems almost overnight by sacrificing some of our luxuries, man is too self-centered to make that his first option, although that reality will ultimately be forced upon future generations. By living in smaller more efficient homes, by giving up our second car, and preparing our food from raw ingredients, we could make room for millions more humans. By paying the price to clean our air and our water, we could provide an abundance for our future generations.

But, instead of looking for the root of our problems, which is our luxurious and wasteful lifestyles, we develop a philosophy that placed the burden of sacrifice on what could, and should be, our future generations.

The American environmental movement, as it is perceived today, is destined to total failure, the reason being its total hypocrisy. It totally ignores our need for personal sacrifice. Instead we place the burden of sacrifice on others.

Too often we see as spokesmen of the environmental movement, movie and T.V. stars, sports stars, wealthy personalities, etc. People, who by virtue of their lifestyles, exemplify the epitome of luxury and waste. So often we hear them make the call for higher taxes to clean up our air and water; we see them protesting the building of power plants, or the drilling of offshore oil wells; they even make movies, for which they are paid millions, to prick the public's environmental consciousness. The hypocrisy of such appeals is so apparent that it is an insult to human intelligence. To my knowledge, there is not one single instance of a movie star, who labels himself an environmental activist, who has demonstrated his willingness to sacrifice his extravagant lifestyle as a first step towards a cleaner environment. If they are not willing to make the real sacrifices required to clean up our environment, how can they have the audacity, to ask it of others?

The environmental movement, as recognized by most Americans today, is a sham. The real cure to our environmental problems has already been implemented, through the collective subconscious of the American people.

Virtually everyone feels that the real cause of our problems is an overpopulation of humans souls, and if this problem isn't addressed, we will all be forced to a life of sacrifice. Once the idea surfaced that humans were too abundant, and we recognized the effects this over abundance exerted on our lives, we started to lose respect for human life.

In our primal history, the bravest and most successful hunter in the tribe was shown the greatest respect. He worked the hardest, and was willing to sacrifice his life to feed his family. Through thousands of years of history, man has earned respect and honor for his ability to provide for his family. Suddenly, that has started to change. Now, the most envied men of our society, are the men who have the most beautiful women, and appear to live a carefree life, filled with wine, woman and song. More and more we hear of women who choose career over motherhood, and those parents who choose to have children often demand that the government share the "burden" of caring for them.

For centuries, our children were treated as treasures, now women ask for the right to abort their babies without need of an explanation. More and more we hear of fathers and mothers mentally and physically abusing their children; of fathers deserting their families; of children being spiritually and physically neglected. We ignore their education, and spend their inheritance. At no time in history have we viewed our fathers and mothers as burdens. Throughout history, our elders were given respect and honor. Today, there are more and more people who feel they should be pushed aside to make room for the younger generation. We are even contemplating the idea of offering our old people a more "dignified" death through euthanasia. What better way to push them aside even quicker, than to offer a philosophy that makes it justifiable? Murders, rapes and human mutilations have become so commonplace that only the most brutal and heinous of these crimes catch our attention. We are human predators, preying off our own kind.

All of this carnage was brought into practice the moment we discovered that there were too many people for the space and resources available. Instead of gold we became dung.

When a leader in the radical group "Earth First" was asked what he thought the optimum human population of Earth should be, he answered;"Zero."
Is it possible that man has "given up" under the mounting burden of world problems and fears, and has let a sense of despair and hopelessness fill his soul?

Is it possible that the animal rights movement is growing in our society because people have lost their sense of direction, and can find no better purpose in life?

Ms. Newkirk's statement; "A rat is a pig is a dog is a boy" does not raise the status of animals, it lowers the dignity of man. It is a step in the collective and subconscious suicide of the human spirit. The concept of animal rights does not raise the quality of the human family, it degrades us to the level of the lowest animal.

Society must recognize the animal rights ideology for the degrading and debilitating sickness it is. A sickness that limits mans potential, destroys his sense of direction and purpose and destroys his spirit. More importantly, it offers no hope for the future of mankind.

The Judeo-Christian faith, as taught in the Bible, has given man HOPE through the promise that neither man, nor God, nor nature will destroy the world.

Gen. 8:22: While the earth remaineth, seed-time and harvest, and cold and heat, and summer and winter, and day and night will not cease.

Not only does the Old Testament give me hope for the future, but I personally have a New Testament hope. In the words of Jesus ...

John 14:1: Let not your heart be troubled; yet believe in God, believe also in me.

It is because of my personal love and respect for nature, that I have spent much of my life in the woods and fields. I continue my life as a hunter and trapper because they are the only ways in which I can be an active participant in the workings of nature. Through this involvement, more than most people of this modern day, I see the destruction and raping of nature caused by a society that doesn't value nature as I do. My only HOPE is in the Biblical promise that although man will be given the power to destroy the world, God will not allow man to destroy his creation. The acceptance of Jesus Christ as my personal savior has given me the PEACE and HOPE I need in this troubled world.

My faith explains and justifies my place in nature ... it doesn't condemn it.

CONCLUSION

A dairy farmer once told me: "If I take care of my animals, they'll take care of me."

No statement better illustrates the association that has grown between man and animals. It is this association that recognizes the fact that the survival of one could very well mean the survival of both.

In our modern, rapidly changing world of sprawling suburbia, fast lifestyles and changing morals, it seems that man wants to break these age old bonds between himself and animals, and force the independence of both. Suddenly man wants to abandon his job as shepherd of the herds, and place the future of all animals back into the hands of nature.

Unfortunately, the very presence of man has destroyed many of the systems and functions of nature. Human societies have changed the face of the earth, polluted her land, air and water, eliminated her checks and balances and ignored her laws.

We have perverted nature to the point where the time has long passed when nature was capable of shepherding the herd. Today, the only shepherds of the flocks are our hunters, trappers and farmers. Without these good shepherds to tend and care for the flocks, they cannot survive alone in a world so dominated and spoiled by man.

By the very destruction of nature, man has shown his ignorance. Must we continue to wallow in ignorance by placing the future of our animals in the hands of people who make their decisions based on emotions rather than knowledge; who want to abandon animals in pursuit of the selfish desire to "raise" human morals; who want to make the final rebellion against nature?

The final decision will be left to the collective wisdom of the American people. It is here, where independence of mind and spirit still flourishes, where the perverted doctrine called "animal rights" must end.

But, before it will end, society must realize that there is a battle being waged to win their hearts and minds; a battle that knows no moral limitations; a battle that serves the motto "the end justifies the means."

Our society must come to understand that our children are being indoctrinated and manipulated into accepting an ideology that is rooted in ignorance, and is a self-serving struggle for a position of power in our society.

As adults, we must not let our emotions rule us, or let a radical fringe group of moral and intellectual elitists dictate our morals. We cannot become like sheep and frantically follow a leader, any leader, over the cliff of desolation.

"What is man without beasts? If the beasts were gone, man would die from a great loneliness of spirit. For whatever happens to the beasts soon happens to man." Chief Seattle, after signing a peace treaty with the U.S. government.

Like any religious cult, the animal rights ideology will continue to have its small band of followers, and they will continue to force their beliefs on our society. They are like some evil weed that sends out its sucker roots, that bond themselves in the fertile grounds of ignorance and misunderstanding. By accepting any PART of the animal rights ideology, you give nourishment to the whole.

Rejection of the animal rights philosophy must involve its total rejection. Instead of accepting animal rights because we agree with one of their doctrines, we must reject all of their doctrines because of the error of even one.

As a trapper recently said: "I wouldn't like the idea of personally having to chop the heads off chickens, or work in the sewers. I'm not one who can work with retarded or terminally ill people. But, I am THANKFUL for those people who are."

The animal rights movement is an attempt to FORCE man's separation from what they view as the EVILS of nature. It is an ideology that turns "man the shepherd" into "man the vicious beast" because they are no longer THANKFUL for the role shepherds play in nature.

ADDENDUM

Russ Carman was born and brought up in a culture which has traditionally revered animals, and used them as a matter of course in daily life. Within the framework of his cultural system is a strict code of ethics which dictates the proper ways in which man and animals co-exist; man does not waste what he has been told is a God-given resource. Man does not mistreat his animals, nor does he confine them cruelly, nor kill them in inhumane ways. "Humane treatment" is defined in that system as treatment which does not cause any more stress or pain than can be helped. American farmers, ranchers, hunters, trappers, veterinarians, wildlife managers and pet owners all traditionally belong to the American culture which has traditionally kept, treated, trained, eaten and profited from animals in one way or another.

None of the members of that culture wants to be forced to give up the traditional relationships with animals, or any of the real benefits of animals use which they feel it is their right to enjoy. Rather recently, these Americans have discovered that there is another cultural tradition taking hold which, if allowed to run its course, would destroy the relationships which man and animals have established, and would eliminate all of man's involvement with animals of any kind.

This "new" idea is a very old one which has been reworked to "fit" with the changing cultural realities. It is called the "animal rights movement" and has increasing numbers supporters, who donate approximately 100 million dollars to the "cause" every year. Most of these supporters are not vegetarians, or the more committed "vegans" (who not only avoid meat, but also avoid using or touching any animal product such as wool, soap, leather, silk, fur, down, milk or eggs). Most supporters of "animal rights" organizations are Americans who still believe that the "movement" is primarily interested in increasing awareness about the need for increased animal welfare. They do not realize that the leaders of this new philosophy are actually working toward a goal of the total elimination of animal use, and are selling the concept through initial campaigns which use "cruelty" as a marketing tool.

Americans are being taught by this movement that there should be no "unnecessary" use of animals for fur. They are now told that they should be ashamed to wear fur because of the synthetic substitutes that are now available. The marketing tool for this has been information which has claimed that trapping wild furbearers is cruel. The same type of information has been given about ranched furbearers; the claim is that they are not well treated, and that they should not be raised "just for the fur." More recently, a campaign has been mounted to insist that veal calves are badly treated because of the necessity of disease-preventing confinement. The ordinary citizen is being taught by the movement to question all farming methods, and many people are now beginning to support legislation to effect the use of antibiotics, hormones and other substances used by modern animal husbandry.

Americans are even beginning to learn to object to the use of animals in medical research, as if all such use was suddenly unjustifiable. All medical researchers are being labelled "vivisectionists" as if their profession was obsessed with intentional torture. Modern science is being dealt a blow which is unjustified, and which could be extremely damaging to the funding of current and future research.

Why is this happening so rapidly? More and more of our population is urban, and only about three percent of Americans are directly involved in animal and grain agriculture, feeding one hundred percent of the rest of the country. Rural Americans do not have the number of congressmen and state representatives which urban and suburban people do; our system of representation is based on population density by election district. Therefore, city people have more state house representatives and congressmen than do rural people. For this reason, urban values are legislated when the normal flow of ideas, values and beliefs does not find acceptance fast enough to suit those who have the most political power.

Russ Carmen describes a trapper's perspective of this process of cultural change, and the cultural shock which rural people are experiencing as city values are forced upon their lives. He has tried to explain what is happening, and how it is affecting good people and the animals which they cling to, and those which are wild and need to be controlled for the common good. Farmers are soon to be affected by this process of artificially forced culture change as are hunters, trappers and the Canadian fisherman-sealers, whose livelihood was so recently damaged at the end of the harp seal pup harvest.

It is no longer going to be useful for animal users to shake their heads, call the animal rightists "crazy" and insist that they will not have an impact because their message is untrue, and therefore, unimportant. Animal lovers and users have got to begin to make a real effort to understand what is happening in this country, before anyone can hope to turn the process around. Russ's book was written to explain the process, to offer reasons why the animals rights movement is anti-social and unjustified and how to overcome the impact of it. His work should be read by every American who has a concern for animals, their welfare and the right of the people to use them humanely and wisely.

Janice S. Henke

BIBLIOGRAPHY

1. George Perkins Marsh, "Man and Nature," edited by David Lowenthal. Cambridge, Mass., Harvard University Press, 1965.

2. The Theory of The Photographic Process. Fourth Edition. Edited by T.H. James. 1977 Macmillan Pub. Co. Inc., 866 Third Ave, New York, NY 10022.

3. "Vegetarianism - A Way of Life. By Dudley Giehl. Page 149.

4. Leo Tolstoy, "Tolstoy, My Father; Reminiscences, Traylmer Maude, Leo Tolstoy, Selected Essays." Modern Library, Random House, 1964 P. 240.

5. Thoreau, Henry David "Walden" Macmillan, 1966, New York.

6. Mohandas K. Gandhi, "The Moral Basis of Vegetarianism." Compiled from Gandhi's writings by R. K. Prabhu, Navajivan Publishing House, 1959, P. 18.

7. Percey Bysshe Shelly, Letter to Leigh and Marianne Hunt, June 29, 1817. Supra Note 47, Vol. 1, P. 543.

8. Forward - Vegetarianism - A Way of Life. Dudley Giehl. Harper & Row, New York, 1979 P. VIII.

9. WLFA, Trapper Magazine, Dec., 1989 (page 24). Quoted from the animal rights magazine "The Animals Agenda."

10. "Vegetarianism - A Way of Life." By Dudley Giehl. Page 149.

11. George Bernard Shaw, "Shaw": An autobiography, 1898-1958 selected from his writings by Stanley Weintraub, Waybright and Talley, 1970, P. 7.

12. Mohandas K. Gandhi: "The Moral Basis of Vegetarianism." Compiled from Gandhi's writings by R. K. Prabhu, Navajivan Publishing House 1959, P. 18.

13. Comments from interview with Dudley Giehl in June, 1975. Found in his book "Vegetarianism - A Way of Life." P. 141 through 145.

14. The Washingtonian/Feb., 1990. "Beyond Cruelty" By Katie McCabe. Page 190.

15. "Vegetarianism - A Way of Life." By Dudley Giehl. Page 125.

REFERENCES.

* ANIMAL LIBERATION. A new ethics for our treatment of animals. By Peter Singer. Avon Books. The Hearst Corp. 105 Madison Ave. New York, NY 10016 Sept. 1977.

* ANIMAL RIGHTS- Considered in Relation to Social Progress. By Henry S. Salt. Published by Society for Animal Rights, Inc. 421 S. State St. Clarks Summit, PA 18411.

* "BEYOND CRUELTY" THE WASHINGTONIAN/ February 1990 issue. Suite 200, 1828 L St. N.W. Washington, D.C. 20036. To the Attn. of Librarian. $3.00 postpaid.

* VEGETARIANISM - A WAY OF LIFE. By Dudley Giehl. Harper & Row. New York 1979.

* DEMOCRACY AND DISOBEDIENCE. Peter Singer. Oxford University Press. 1973.

* INCURABLY Ill FOR ANIMAL RESEARCH. P.O. Box 1873, Bridgeview, IL 60455.

* RETURNING TO EDEN. By Michael W. Fox. The Viking Press, 625 Madison Ave. New York, NY 10022.

* SEAL WARS! An American Viewpoint. By Janice Scott Henke. Breakwater Books Ltd., 277 Duckworth Street. St. John's, Newfoundland, A1C 1G9.

— ORDER FORM —

Order your additional copies here of <u>The Illusions Of Animal Rights</u> by author Russ Carman.

Photocopy this form, send all necessary information on a separate sheet of paper or fill out this form and send with payment to the address below.

Yes, I would like to receive additional copies of Russ Carman's book <u>The Illusions Of Animal Rights.</u>

( ) Send me _____ books at $12.95 per issue plus $1.50 per book for postage and handling in the U.S.

( ) Send me _____ books at $12.95 per issue plus $5.00 per book for postage and handling outside of the U.S.

Name _____

Address _____

City _____

State _____ Zip _____

Send to:
Krause Publications, Inc.
Outdoor Books Division
700 E. State St., Iola, WI 54990
Phone: 715-445-2214

-NOTES-

-NOTES-

-NOTES-

-NOTES-